THE KING'S HIGHWAY

THE
KING'S HIGHWAY

OPENED AND CLEARED

A SELECTION OF CHOICE **Sermons** DELIVERED IN LONDON

BY

C. H. SPURGEON

CHRISTIAN FOCUS
PUBLICATIONS

This edition
published by

Houston   Christian Focus   Tain
Texas   Publications   Ross-shire
U.S.A.   Scotland

Printed and bound in Great Britain by
Richard Clay Ltd, Bungay, Suffolk

Preface

THIS volume of Sermons is sent forth to the world with the Author's heartiest thanksgivings, and sincerest prayers Years of public ministry amid thronging multitudes supply the most blessed recollections. The faithfulness of God, the fellowship of Christ, the comforts of the Spirit, the power of prayer, the prevalence of faith, the force of truth, the glory of the Gospel, and other kindred Heaven-born truths, have received plentiful illustrations in our experience, for which we would render our joyous praise. Preserved in Jesus amid daily temptations, supplied with strength for incessant labours, guided through singular difficulties, and comforted under ferocious attacks, we can sing unto the Lord who hath been at our right hand in every time of need. The All-sufficiency of God we have joyously proved, while the insufficiency of the creature we have painfully felt. Vain is the help of man, but glorious is the right arm of the Most High.

These discourses are purely extempore, and although reported with singular accuracy, as there are no manuscripts with which to compare the reports, errors will creep in. As to the preacher's style, he who expects elaboration and exact accuracy in an extempore discourse, and especially in a report printed the next day, and published the next, deserves to be disappointed.

In the matter of Gospel doctrine, we trust no reader will perceive any variation. No new gospel have we aimed to declare. More faith is needed, but not a new creed " a firmer confidence, but not a better covenant; a stronger trust, but not a more solid foundation. Developments, discoveries, and theorisings, we are content to leave to those who, having never tasted the old wine, are naturally thirsty for the new. Our colours are nailed to the mast, and in doctrine we take for our motto, *"Semper idem."* We are foolish enough to be content with the old theology, and even to believe it incapable of improvement.

One thing alone places this book above contempt—and that accomplishes the deed so triumphantly, that the preacher defies the opinion of man—it is the fact, that to his certain knowledge, there is scarce a Sermon here which has not been stamped by the hand of the Almighty, by the conversion of a soul. Some single Sermons here have been, under God, the means of the salvation of not less than twenty souls; at least, that number have come under the preacher's notice from one Sermon only; and doubtless more shall be discovered at the last day.

It is our custom to mention, for the guidance of those who distribute these sermons, those which have been most signally owned in the salvation of the sinners. There are several which have been exceedingly prolific. *"The King's Highway Opened and Cleared"* has brought very many to comfort of soul and decision for Christ. Both in the hearing and reading of it, men who were both timorous and ignorant have found grace to walk in the Lord's way. Unto the gracious Spirit be glory. *"God's First Words to the First Sinner"* has been blessed. The sermon, *"None But Jesus,"* has been translated for the Aborigines of New Zealand, and some thousands have been distributed. The reading of this sermon in Auckland, New Zealand, has led to several conversions among Europeans and natives.

During the past year, two hundred thousand copies of our sermons have been presented to the Universities of Cambridge and Oxford.

The Head of the Church has opened up to us another door of usefulness, in the translation of these sermons into the *Swedish* tongue, in which language they have found a very wide circulation; so that we speak in *English*, *French*, *Welsh*, *Dutch*, *German*, *Italian*, *Swedish*, and almost all the Protestant languages.

C. H. Spurgeon

Contents

Introduction

TO A VOLUME OF SELECTED SERMONS BY C. H. SPURGEON

BY

Sir William Robertson Nichol

THIS volume contains sermons preached by C. H. SPURGEON in London. His first sermon in London was preached in New Park Street Chapel on December 18, 1853. He was then little more than nineteen years old, having been born at Kelvedon, Essex, on June 19, 1834. Young as he was, this first sermon in London was the 673rd that he had preached. When he came to New Park Street Chapel the congregation was greatly reduced in numbers, and almost on the point of dissolution. Very soon, however, it was densely crowded, and while it was being enlarged the congregation met in Exeter Hall, where many of these sermons were preached. The enlarged chapel when opened proved too small, and the Metropolitan Tabernacle was projected.

Mr. Spurgeon's career in the Metropolitan Tabernacle to his death in 1892 has no parallel in the history of the pulpit. To the end the place was crowded by some 6000 hearers at every Sunday service. Considering that some of the sermons here published were preached by a young man of twenty-one, their maturity is amazing. The youth was from the first a ripe theologian, master of a great system of thought, definite and precise in his teaching. It is little to say that he did not shrink from great themes; from the first he chose them by preference.

In their printed form his sermons have had an unprecedented circulation, and they will long survive him. Their strong, racy, Saxon English style, their theological grasp, their evangelical earnestness, their rich and homely wisdom, and their amazing fertility of thought within the limits which the preacher resolutely prescribes for himself, give them a separate place in the literature of the pulpit.   W. R. N.

THE KING'S HIGHWAY

God's First Words to the First Sinner

"The Lord God called unto Adam, and said unto him, Where art thou?" (Genesis 3. 9).

ADAM ought to have sought out his Maker. He should have gone through the garden crying for his God, "My God, my God, I have sinned against Thee. Where art *Thou*? Low at Thy feet Thy creature falls and asks mercy at Thy hands. I confess Thy justice and beseech Thy mercy, if mercy can be shown to such an one as I am."

Instead thereof, Adam flies from God. The sinner comes not to God; God comes to him. It is not, "My God, where art Thou?" but the first cry is the voice of grace, "Sinner, where art *thou*?" God comes to man; man seeks not his God. There has never been found from Adam's day until now a single instance in which the sinner *first* sought his God. God must first seek him. The sheep strays of itself, but it never returns to its fold unless sought by the Great Shepherd. It is human to err, it is **Divine to repent.** Man *can* commit iniquity, but even to know that it is iniquity so as to feel the guilt of it, is the gift of the grace of God.

The question which the Lord asked of Adam may be used in five different ways, for there is always in the utterance of the Divine One a great depth which coucheth beneath. Our words, if they give one sense, do well; but the Lord knoweth how to speak so that He shall teach many truths in few words. We give little in much: God giveth much in little.

I. We believe that the inquiry of God was intended

In an Arousing Sense—

"Adam, where art thou?" Sin stultifies the conscience, it drugs the mind, so that after sin man is not so capable of understanding his danger as he would have been without it. Sin is a poison which kills conscience painlessly by mortification. Men die by sin, as men die when frozen to death upon the Alps—they die in a sleep; they sleep, and sleep, and sleep, and sleep on, till death closes the scene, and then in hell they awake in torments. One of the first works of grace in a man is to put aside this sleep, to startle him from his lethargy, to make him open his eyes and discover his danger. One of the first deeds of the good physician is to put sensibility into our flesh. It has become

cold, and dead, and mortified; He puts life into it, and then there is pain; but that very pain has a salutary effect upon us.

Adam had perceived in some degree into what a state his sin had brought him, but this question was meant to stir the depths of his spirit, and wake him up to such a sense of danger, that he should labour to escape from the wrath to come. *"Adam, where art thou?"*—look at thyself now, naked, a stranger to thy God, dreading the presence of thy Maker, miserable, undone. *"Adam, where art thou?"*—with a hard heart, with a rebellious will, fallen, fallen, fallen from thy high estate. *"Adam, where art thou?"* Lost! lost to thy God, lost to happiness, lost to peace, lost in time, lost in eternity. *Sinner, "where art thou?"*

"Where art thou?" Thy life is frail; nothing can be more weak. A spider's line is a cable compared with the thread of thy life. Dreams are substantial masonry compared with the bubble structure of thy being. Thou art here and thou art gone. Thou sittest here to-day; ere another week is past thou mayest be lost in another world. Oh, where art thou, man? Unpardoned, and yet a dying man! Condemned, yet going carelessly towards destruction!

If we fear that our personal estates are at all in

jeopardy we have anxious nights and toilsome days; but, oh! our souls—our poor, poor souls—we play with them as if they were worthless counters, or bits of platter, which a child might pick up in the streets and cast away! Sinner! is thy soul so poor a bauble that thou canst afford to lose it, because thou wilt not break thy sleep and stay thy pleasurable dreams! Oh, if a brother's heart can move thy heart, and if a brother's voice can wake thy sleeping eyes, I would say, "What aileth thee, O sleeper? Arise, and call upon thy God! Awake! why sleepest thou? Awake to answer the question, 'Where art thou?'—lost, ruined, and undone! O sinner, where art thou?"

II. The question was meant to

Convince of Sin,

and so to lead to a confession. Had Adam's heart been in a right state, he would have made a full confession of his sinfulness. *"Where art thou?"* Let us hear the voice of God saying that to us, if to-day we are out of God and out of Christ. "Where art thou, Adam? I made thee in Mine own image, I made thee a little lower than the angels: I made thee to have dominion over the works of My hands: I put all things under thy feet—the fowl of the air, and the fish of the sea, and whatsoever passeth through the depths of the sea. I gave this whole garden of delight to be thy home. I honoured thee with My presence, I thought of thy welfare, and forestalled all thy desires. The moon did not hurt thee by night; the sun did not smite thee by day. I tempered the winds for thee; I clothed the trees with fruit for thy nourishment. I made all things minister to thy happiness. *Where art thou?* I asked of thee but that little thing that thou wouldest not touch one tree which I had reserved for Myself. *Where art thou?* Art thou in the room of a thief, a rebel, a traitor? Hast thou sinned? O Adam, where art thou?"

And now, sinner, hear me. "Where art thou?" To many of you the Lord might say, "I gave you a godly mother who wept over you in your childhood; gave you a holy father who longed for your conversion. I gave you the gift of Providence—you never wanted for a meal. I clothed your back. I put you in a comfortable position in life. I raised you up from a bed of sickness. I overlooked ten thousand follies. My mercies like a river have flown to you. When you opened your eyes in the morning, it was to look upon My goodness; and till the last moment of the night I was your helper, and drew the curtain about your

defenceless head.   I have covered thee with My
feathers, under My wings hast thou trusted, and now
where art thou?   Hast thou not forgotten My commandments, abhorred My Person, broken My laws,
rejected My Son?   Art thou not at this day a dis-
believer, content to trust to thine own works, but not
to take the finished righteousness of My beloved Son,
the Saviour of the world?   What hast thou done for
Him who has done so much for thee?   *Where art thou*?
Art thou not to-day in the camp of My enemy?   Art
thou not on Satan's side, defying Me, and lifting up
the puny arm of thy rebellion against the Lord that
made thee, and that keepeth the breath in thy nostrils
—in whose hand thy life is, and whose are all thy
ways?   Sinner, *where art thou*?   After all God's goodness—still a sinner!"

III. The third way in which we may regard the
question: The Lord God called unto Adam, and said
unto him, "Where art thou?"   We may regard this
text as the VOICE OF GOD

Bemoaning Man's Lost Estate.

It is as if God uttered the words of the prophet,
"How can I give thee up?   How can I utterly destroy
thee?   How can I set thee as Admah?   How shall I

make thee as Zeboim? Where art thou my poor Adam? Thou didst talk with Me, but thou hast now fled from Me. Thou wast happy once, what art thou now? Naked, and poor, and miserable. Thou wast once in My image glorious, blessed, where art thou now? Poor Adam, where art thou?"

And now have I here any soul on whom the former part of the text has had some effect? Do you feel yourself to be lost, and do you discern that this lostness is the result of your own wilful folly? Do you bemoan yourself? Ah, then, God bemoans you. He is saying to you who are now weeping over sin, "Ah, poor child, what pain thou sufferest from thine own wilful folly!" A father's bowels move; he longs to clasp his Ephraim to his breast. Do not think, sinner, that God is stony-hearted. *Thou* hast a heart of stone, God has not. Do not think that He is slow to move: *thou* art slow to move—*He* is not.

Soul, let not Satan deceive thee by telling thee that God is hard, unkind, unwilling to forgive! Try Him! Just as thou art—black, filthy, self-condemned; and if thou needest anything to make thee try Him, hear again the Lord's plaintive cry, as it rings through the trees of Eden, "Adam, My own creature, where, *where art thou*?"

2

IV. But now I must turn to a fourth way in which no doubt this verse was intended, It is an arousing voice, a convincing voice, a bemoaning voice; but, in the fourth place, it is

A Seeking Voice.

"Adam, where art thou?" I am come to find thee, wherever thou mayest be. I will look for thee, till the eyes of My pity see thee. I will follow thee till the hand of My mercy reaches thee; and I will still hold thee till I bring thee back to Myself, and reconcile thee to My heart.

Again, if you have been able to follow me through the three parts of the discourse, I can speak confidently to you. You who are lost, perishing sinners, hear the voice of God, for it speaks to you. *"Where art thou?"* for I am come to seek thee. "Lord, I am in such a place that I cannot do anything for myself." "Then I am come to seek thee and do all for thee." "Lord, I am in such a place that the law threatens me and justice frowns upon me." "I am come to answer the threatenings of the law, and to bear all the wrath of justice." "Oh, but I have sinned beyond all hope." "Yes, but I have come to give hope to hopeless sinners." "Aye, but then I deserve to be lost." "Yes, but I have come to magnify the law and make it honourable, and so to give thee thy deserts in the person of Christ, and then to give thee My mercy because of *His* merits." There is not a sinner here conscious of his lost estate who can be in a position out of which he cannot be brought. I will conceive the worst of all the worst, the vilest of all the vile; we will bring up those who have taken high degrees in the devil's synagogue and become masters of iniquity; but still if with the tearful eye they look alone to the wounds of Him who shed His blood for sinners, He is able also to save them to the uttermost that come unto God by Him.

V. Lastly, we feel sure that this text may be used, and must be used, in another sense. To those who reject the text, as a voice of arousing and conviction, to those who despise it as the voice of mercy bemoaning them, or as the voice of goodness seeking them, it comes in another way; it is the voice of

Justice Summoning Them.

Adam had fled, but God must have him come to His bar. *"Where art thou*, Adam? Come hither, man, come hither; I must judge thee, sin cannot go unpunished. Come, and thy guilty spouse with thee.

Come hither; I must put questions to thee; I must hear thy pleadings, and since they will be vain and void I must pronounce thy sentence." For though there was much of pity in the question, there was something of severity, too. "Adam, Adam, *where art thou*? Come thou hither to be judged."

To-day you hear not that cry; it is mercifully postponed. You shall hear it soon; you shall hear it for the first time, like mutterings of thunder when the storm begins; when sickness casts thee on thy bed, and death looks through his bony eyes upon thee, and touches thee with his ghastly hand, and saith, "Prepare to meet thy God." Thou mayest put off the question to-day; thou wilt have to deal with it then, when God Himself shall come into closer contact with thy nature, than He doth to-day. Thou shalt contend with the pains of sickness or disease; but there shall be a direr pain than these. Thou shalt have to look on death; but death shall not be the most terrible of all thy terrors, for thou shalt see behind death the judgment and the doom. *Then* thou wilt hear it, when the room is silent, and voices of wife and child are hushed; when only the clock is ticking, thou shalt hear the footfalls of God coming to thee in the eventide of thy life, and saying to thee, "*Where art thou*?

Now thou shalt meet Me.   Gird up thy loins!   No invitation of mercy for thee more; thy day of mercy is gone.   Now thou shalt meet Me face to face. " "*Where art thou?*"

Canst thou brag and boast now, when thy nerves have become roads for the hot feet of pain to travel on, and thy strength has gone and fled, and thou art as a candle ready to die out?   Where now thine oaths? Where now thy merry-making and thy jests?   Where art thou now?   You may toss and turn; but you will not be able to escape the question; you will try to look back to this life, but you will be compelled to look forward to the life or the death to come; and still will the Lord whisper into your ears, "*Where art thou?*"

Then shall come the last struggle, when the strong man shall be bowed, when the bright and glittering eye shall be covered o'er with film, and the tongue shall cleave to the roof of the mouth, and the hand shall lie strengthless on the bed, and the feet shall no more be able to support the body; when the pulse shall fail, and the clammy death-sweat shall stand upon the brow; and in those last moments there will still be heard that awful voice, rising with the gathering storm till it reaches the full grandeur of the awful tempest—"*Where art thou?*"   In the Jordan without

God; nearing the grave without hope; dying, but no Christ to help thee; launching upon eternity, but no hope of eternal salvation.

It is over; and the last pang has passed, and the thread is snapped that bound the spirit to the body, and you are gone into another world. But the question follows you—*"Where art thou?"* Thy spirit is now awake; it sleeps no more; it is rid of the dull flesh that kept it sullen, stolid, stupid, dead. Now it hears that voice, indeed, and it thrills through and through the spirit, for the soul is brought before its God. *"Where art thou?"* "Where are thou?" cries the quickened conscience; and God answers it, "Depart, thou cursed one!" The spirit departs from God, not to hide itself among the trees of the garden, but to plunge itself into waves of agony.

And now many years have passed, and the body, though the soul has been alive and has suffered, has been sleeping in the grave, and the worms have devoured it. But hark! the Day of judgment, the day of thunder has arrived, shrill above all thunders sounds the awful trump; and after the trumpet comes the voice—"Awake, ye dead, and come to judgment!" Amidst that awful tumult is heard the cry, *"Where art thou?"* The angelic messenger has found out *your* body, and from the grave your body starts, from underneath the green sward. Up it leaps in answer to the question, *"Where art thou?"* and to its horror, its ghastly spirit comes back; its soul, that long has suffered, returns into the resurrection body, and they twain, comrades in sin, are now companions in judgment. The cry rings forth, and that very ear shall hear it that now listens to me—*"Where art thou?"*

Then comes the great white throne, and those very eyes shall see it that now gaze on me; and then comes the commencement of the dread assize—and that heart shall quail then which moves not now. Then shall come your own personal trial; and oh! sinner, sinner, it is not for me to describe your terror. I could not give even the faintest picture of that death-sound, and of the death of your immortal spirit while you hear it: "I was an hungered and ye gave Me no meat; I was thirsty and ye gave Me no drink; inasmuch as ye did it not unto one of the least of these My brethren ye did it not to Me; and these shall go away into everlasting punishment, but the righteous into life eternal"

"Oh, earth! earth! earth! hear the word of the Lord," I pray each of you to hear it for yourselves. I have not talked to you of dreams. You know they are realities; and if you know it not now you shall ere long. I do beseech you by the Blood of Him that died for sinners—and what stronger argument can I use?—think of the question, *"Where art thou?"* May God show you where you are. Hear the bemoaning voice of God, as pityingly He weeps over you. Seek His face, for He seeks you; and then you need not dread to hear Him say at the last, *"Where art thou?"* but you will be able to say, "Here am I, and the children Thou hast given me. We have washed our robes, and made them white in the Blood of the Lamb; and, Father, here we are, hoping to dwell in Thy presence for ever and ever."

Oh, that I could plead with you as a man pleadeth for his life! Would that these lips of clay were lips of fire, and this tongue no more of flesh, but a live coal taken with the tongs from off the altar! Oh! for words that would burn their way into your souls! O sinner, sinner, why wilt thou die? Why wilt thou perish? Man, eternity is an awful thing, and to meet an angry God is dreadful, and to be judged and condemned, what tongue can tell the horror. Escape for thy life; look not behind thee; stay not in all the plain; escape to Mount Calvary, lest thou be consumed. "Believe on the Lord Jesus Christ;" trust Him with thy soul; trust Him with it *now*, "and thou shalt be saved."

The Old, Old Story

"In due time Christ died for the ungodly" (Rom. 5. 6).

THE doctrine of the atonement is very simple. It just consists in the substitution of Christ in the place of the sinner; Christ being treated as if he were the sinner, and then the transgressor being treated as if he were the righteous one. It is a change of persons; Christ becomes the sinner; He stands in the sinner's place and stead; He was numbered with the transgressors; the sinner becomes righteous; he stands in Christ's place and stead, and is numbered with the righteous ones. Christ has no sin of His own, but He takes human guilt, and is punished for human folly. We have no righteousness of our own, but we take the Divine righteousness; we are rewarded for it, and stand accepted before God as though that righteousness had been wrought out by ourselves. "In due time Christ died for the ungodly" (Rom. 5. 6), that He might take away their sins.

It is not my present object to prove this doctrine. There is no need to be always arguing what we know to be *true*. Rather let us say a few earnest words by way of *commending this doctrine of the atonement*; and afterwards I shall propound it *by way of application*.

I. First, then,

By Way of Commendation.

1. Our first commendation on the doctrine of the atonement is, that it commends itself **to the understanding**. The way-faring man, though his intellect be but one grade beyond an idiot, may get a hold on the truth of substitution without any difficulty. If you perish, it will not be because the Gospel was beyond your comprehension. If you go down to Hell, it will not be because you were not able to understand how God can be just, and yet the justifier of the ungodly.

When Mr. Kilpin was once preaching a very good and earnest sermon, he used the word "Deity," and a sailor sitting down below leaned forward and said, "Beg your pardon, sir, but who's he, pray? Do you mean God Almighty?" "Yes," said Mr. Kilpin, "I do mean God, and I ought not to have used a word which you could not understand." "I thank you, sir," said the sailor, and looked as of he would devour the rest of the sermon in the interest which he felt in it even to the close. Now that one unvarnished fact is but an index of that which prevails in every land.

A doctrine of atonement that is not simple, a doctrine which needs a man to be a great scholar before he can comprehend it himself, and to be a still greater adept before he can tell it to others—such a doctrine is manifestly not of God, because it is not suited to God's creatures. It is fascinating to one in a thousand of them, but it is not suited to those poor of this world who are rich in faith; not suited to those babes to whom God has revealed the things of the Kingdom while He has hidden them from the wise and prudent.

2. Nor is this doctrine of the atonement to be commended merely for its simplicity, but because while suiting the understanding if also **suits the conscience**. How it satisfies the conscience no tongue can tell! When a man is awakened and his conscience stings him, when the Spirit of God has shown him his sin and his guilt, there is nothing but the Blood of Christ that can ever give him peace. Peter might have stood up at the prow of the boat and have said to the winds and to the waves, "Peace, be still," but they would have gone on roaring with unabated fury.

When ROBERT HALL first went to Cambridge to preach, the Cambridge folks were nearly Unitarians.

So he preached upon the doctrine of the finished work
of Christ, and some of them came to him in the vestry
and said, "Mr. Hall, this will never do." "Why
not?" said he, "Why, your sermon was only fit for
old women." "And why only fit for old women?"
said Mr. Hall. "Because," said they, "they are
tottering on the border of the grave, and they want
comfort, and, therefore, it will suit them, but it will
not do for us." "Very well," said Mr. Hall, "you
have unconsciously paid me all the compliment that
I can ask for; if this is good for old women on the
borders of the grave, it must be good for you if you are
in your right senses, for *the borders of the grave is where
we all stand.*"

A Gospel without an atonement may do very well
for young ladies and gentlemen who do not know that
they ever did anything wrong. It will just suit your
lackadaisical people who have not got a heart for any-
body to see; who have always been quite moral,
upright, and respectable; who would feel insulted if
you told them they deserved to be sent to Hell; who
would not for a moment allow that they could be
depraved or fallen creatures. But let a man be really
guilty and know it; let him be really awake to his lost
state, and I aver that none but Jesus—none but Jesus,

nothing but the precious Blood can give him peace
and rest.

For these two things, then, commend us to the
doctrine of the atonement, because it suits the understanding of the most lowly, and will quiet the conscience of the most troubled.

3. It has, moreover, this peculiar excellency, that
it softens the heart. There is a mysterious softening
and melting power in the story of the sacrifice of
Christ. I know a dear Christian woman who loved her
little ones and sought their salvation. When she
prayed for them she thought it right to use the best
means she could to arrest their attention and awaken
their mind. The means, however, which she thought
best calculated for her object was the terrors of the
Lord. She used to read to her children chapter after
chapter of *Alleine's Alarm to the Unconverted*. But
the boy's heart grew hardened, as if it were annealed
rather than melted by the furnace of fear. The ham-
mer welded the heart to sin, but did not break it.
But when he heard of Jesus' love to His people,
though he feared he was not one of His people, still
it used to make him weep to think Jesus should love
anybody after such a sort. Even now that he has come
to manhood, law and terrors make him dead and

stolid, but Thy Blood Jesus, Thine agonies in Gethsemane and on the tree, he cannot bear; they melt
him, his soul flows through his eyes in tears; he weeps
himself away from grateful love to Thee for what Thou
hast done.

It is because Christ suffered for my sins, because He
was condemned that I might be acquitted, and not be
punished as the result of my guilt: it is this that makes
His sufferings such a cordial to my heart.

> "See on the bloody tree,
>   The illustrious sufferer hangs,
> The torments due to thee,
>   He bore the dreadful pangs;
> And cancelled there, the mighty sum,
> Sins present, past, and sins to come.'"

There is a melting power here which is not to be found
in all the world besides.

4. I will detain you yet once more on this point.
We commend the doctrine of the atonement because,
besides suiting the understanding, quieting the conscience, and melting the heart, we know there is a
power in it to **affect the outward life**. No man can
believe that Christ suffered for his sins and yet live
in sin. No man can believe that his iniquities were
the murderers of Christ, and yet go and hug those
murderers to his bosom. The proof, after all, is in
the trial.

I knew a village once that was perhaps one of the worst villages in England for many things; where many an illicit still was yielding its noxious liquor to a manufacturer without payment of the duty to the Government, and where, in connection with that, all manner of riot and iniquity were rife. There went a lad into that village, and but a lad, and one who had no scholarship, but was rough, and sometimes vulgar. He began to preach there, and it pleased God to turn that village upside down, and in a short time the little thatched chapel was crammed, and the biggest vagabonds of the village were weeping floods of tears, and those who had been the curse of the parish became its blessing; and where there had been robberies and villanies of every kind all round the neighbourhood, there were none, because the men who did the mischief were themselves in the house of God, rejoicing to hear of Jesus crucified. Mark me, I am not telling you an exaggerated story now, nor a thing that I do not know. Yet this one thing I remember to the praise of God's grace, it pleased the Lord to work signs and wonders in our midst. He showed the power of Jesus' Name, and made us witnesses to that Gospel which can win souls, draw reluctant hearts, and mould the life and conduct of men afresh.

II. Secondly, one or two points

By Way of Exhortation.

Christian man, you believe that your sins are for
given, and that Christ has made a full atonement
for them.   What shall we say to you?

1. To you first we say, what **a joyful Christian
you ought to be**! How you should live above the
common trials and troubles of the world! Since sin
is forgiven, what matter what happens to you now?
Luther said, "Smite, Lord, smite, for my sin is forgiven; if Thou hast but forgiven me, smite as hard as
Thou wilt;" as if he felt like a child who had done
wrong, and cared not how his father might whip him
if he would but forgive him.   So *I* think you can say,
"Send sickness, poverty, losses, crosses, slander,
persecution, what Thou wilt, Thou hast forgiven me,
and my soul is glad, and my spirit is rejoiced."

2. And, again, Christian, if this be true that there
is an atonement made for sin, **tell it, tell it, tell it**.
"We cannot all preach," say you; no, but tell it,
tell it.   "I could not prepare a sermon;" tell it; tell
out the story; tell out the mystery and wonder of
Christ's love. "But I should never get a congregation;"
tell it in your house; tell it by the fire-side.   "But I
have none but little children;" tell it to your children,

and let them know the sweet mystery of the Cross, and the blessed history of Him who lived and died for sinners. Tell it, for you know not into what ears you may speak. Tell it often, for thus will you have the better hope that you may turn sinners to Christ. Lacking talent, lacking the graces of oratory, be glad that you lack these, and glory in your infirmity that the power of Christ may rest upon you, but do tell it.

3. Again, to another class of you, this word. If God has in Christ made an atonement and opened a way of salvation, **what must be your guilt** who try to open another way; who say, "I will be good and virtuous; I will attend to ceremonies; I will save myself?" Fool that thou art, thou hast insulted God in His tenderest point, for thou hast insulted His Son. Thou hast said, "I can do it without that Blood;" thou hast, in fact, trampled on the Blood of Christ, and said, "I need it not." Oh, if the sinner who repents not be lost, with what accumulated terrors shall he be lost, who, in addition to his impenitence, heaps affronts upon the Person of Christ by going about to establish his own righteousness. Leave it; leave your rags, you will never make a garment of them; leave that pilfered treasure of thine; it is a counterfeit; forsake it. I counsel thee to buy

3

of Christ fine raiment, that thou mayest be clothed, and fine gold that thou mayest be rich.

4. And consider this, one and all of you, oh my hearers! If Christ hath made atonement for the ungodly, then let the question go round, let it echo in every heart, and let it be repeated by every lip: "**Why not for me?**" and "Why not *for me*?" Hope, sinner, hope; he died for the ungodly. If it had said He died for the *godly*, there were no hope for thee. If it had been written that He died to save the *good*, the excellent, and the perfect, then thou hast no chance. He died for the *ungodly*; thou art such an one; what reason hast thou to conclude that He did not die for Thee? Hark thee, man; this is what Christ saith to thee: "Believe, and thou shalt be saved;" that is, trust, and thou shalt be saved. Trust thy soul in the hands of Him who carried thy load upon the Cross; trust Him now. You have nothing else to trust to; hang on Him. You are going down; you are going down. The waves are gathering about you, and soon shall they swallow you up, and we shall hear your gurglings as you sink. See, He stretches out His hand. "Sinner," saith He, "I will bear thee up; though Hell's fiery waves should dash against thee I will bear thee through them all, only trust Me.

What sayest thou, sinner? Wilt thou trust Him? Oh, my soul, recollect the moment when first I trusted in Him There is joy in Heaven over one sinner that repenteth, but I hardly think that is greater joy than the joy of the repenting sinner when he first finds Christ. So simply and so easy it seemed to me when I came to know it. I had only to look and live, only to trust and be saved. Year after year had I been running about hither and thither to try and do what was done beforehand, to try and get ready for that which did not want any readiness. Oh, happy was that day when I ventured to step in by the open door of His mercy, to sit at the table of grace ready spread, and to eat and drink, asking no questions! Oh, soul, do the same! Take courage. Trust Christ, and if he cast thee away when thou hast trusted Him—my soul for thine as we meet at the bar of God, I will be pawn and pledge for thee at the last great Day if such thou needest; but He cannot and He will not cast out any that come to Him by faith. May God now accept and bless us all, for Jesus' sake! Amen.

The Friend of Sinners

"He was numbered with the transgressors; and he bare the sin of many, and made intercession for the transgressors" (Isa. 53. 12).

OUR text, in its threefold character, shows the intimate connection which exists between Jesus and sinners, for in none of its sentences is there meaning unless there be a sinner, and unless Christ has come into connection with him. Bring in a company of righteous people who think they have no sin and they cannot appreciate the text; in fact it can have no meaning to them.

I. We shall begin then, by taking the first sentence. To the sinner, troubled and alarmed on account of guilt, there will be much comfort in the thought that

Christ is Enrolled Among Sinners.

"HE WAS NUMBERED WITH THE TRANSGRESSORS."

1. He was numbered with them, first, **in the census of the Roman Empire**. There went out a decree from Caesar Augustus that all the world should be taxed, and the espoused wife of Joseph, being great

with child, must travel to Bethlehem that Christ may
be born there, and that He may be numbered with the
transgressing people who, for their sins, were subject
to the Roman yoke.

2. Years rolled on, and that child who had been
early numbered with transgressors, and had received
the seal of transgression in the circumcision, which
represents the putting away of the flesh—that child,
having come to manhood, goes forth into the world
and is numbered with transgressors **in the scroll of
Fame**. Ask public rumour, "What is the character
of Jesus of Nazareth?" and it cannot find a word in its
vocabulary foul enough for him. "This ——," they
sometimes said; and our translators have inserted the
word "fellow" because in the original there is an
ellipsis, the evangelists, I suppose, hardly liking to
write the word which had been cast upon Christ Jesus.
Fame, with her lying tongue, said He was a drunken
man and a wine-bibber, because He would not yield
to the asceticism of the age. They called Him mad.
His warm enthusiasm, His stern and unflinching
rebukes of wickedness in high places, brought upon
Him the accusation that He had a devil. "Thou hast
a devil and art mad," said they. They called the
Master of the house Beelzebub! Even the drunkards

made Him their song, and the vilest thought Him
viler than themselves, for He was, by current rumour,
numbered with the transgressors.

3. But to make the matter still more forcible, "he
was numbered with transgressors **in the courts of
law.**" The ecclesiastical court of Judaism, the
Sanhedrin, said of Him, "Thou blasphemest;" and
they smote Him on the cheek.

4. Then, **the whole Jewish people numbered
Him** with transgressors; nay, they reprobated Him
as a more abominable transgressor than a thief and a
murderer who had excited sedition.　Barabbas is put
in competition with Christ, and they say, "Not this
Man, but Barabbas." His being numbered with
transgressors is no fiction.　Lo, He bears the transgressor's scourging!　He is tied to the whipping-post,
His back is marred and scarred; the ploughers make
deep furrows, and the Blood flows in streams.　He is
numbered with transgressors, for He bears the felon's
Cross; He comes into the street bowed down with
the weight of His own gibbet, which He must carry
upon His raw and bleeding shoulders; He goes along
to the place of doom; He comes to Calvary—the place
of a skull—and there, hoisted upon the Cross, hanging
in mid-air, as if earth rejected Him and Heaven

refused Him shelter, He dies the ignominious death of the Cross and is thus numbered with transgressors.

But will there be none to enter a protest? Will no eye pity? Will no man declare His innocence? None; they are all silent! Silent, did I say? 'Tis worse! All earth holds up its hands for his death; it is carried unanimously. Jew and Gentile, bond and free, they are all there. They thrust out the tongue; they hoot; they laugh; they cry, "Let Him deliver Him, seeing He delighted in Him." His Name is written in the calendar of crime by the whole universe; for He is despised and rejected of men; *of all men* is He accounted to be the off-scouring of all things, and is put to grief.

But will not Heaven interfere? O God, upon Thy throne, wilt Thou let the innocent suffer? He is fast nailed to the tree, and cries in agony, "I thirst." Wilt Thou permit this Man to be numbered with transgressors? *Is it rightly done?* It is; Heaven confirms it. He has no sin of His own, but He has the sin of His people upon His shoulders; and God, the Eternal Judge, shows that He, too, considers Him to be in the roll of transgressors, for He veils His face; and the Eternal Father betakes Him to His hiding-place, and Christ can neither see a smile nor a glance of His Father's face, till He shrieks in agony so unutterable, that the words cannot express the meaning of the Redeemer's soul: "My God, My God, why hast Thou forsaken Me?" The only answer from Heaven being, "I must forsake transgressors; *Thou art numbered with them*, and therefore, I must forsake Thee."

But surely the doom will not be fulfilled? Certainly, He will be taken down ere He dies? Death is the curse for sin; it cannot come on any but transgressors; it is impossible for the innocent to die, as impossible as for immortality to be annihilated. Surely, then, the Lord will deliver His Son at the last moment, and having tried Him in the furnace, He will bring Him out? Nay, not so; He must become obedient unto death, *even the death of the Cross*.

He died without a protest on the part of earth, or Heaven, or Hell; He that was numbered with the transgressors, having worn the transgressor's crown of thorns, lies in the transgressor's grave. "He made His grave with the wicked, and with the rich in His death; because He had done no violence, neither was any deceit in His mouth."

It is a marvellous thing, brethren, a marvellous thing! Who ever heard of an angel being numbered

with devils? Who ever heard of Gabriel being numbered with fiends? But this is more marvellous than
that would be. Here is the Son of God numbered,
not with the sons of men (that were a gracious act),
but numbered with transgressors; numbered, not
with the faithful who struggle after purity; numbered,
not with those who repel temptation and resist sin;
numbered, not with those who earn unto themselves
a good degree and much boldness in the faith—that
were a marvellous condescension; but here it is
written, "He was numbered *with the transgressors.*"

Oh soul, can thy heart say, "Then if He was numbered with *me*, if He put His Name down where mine
stands in that terrific roll, then I will believe in Him
that He is able and willing to save *me*, and I will
trust my soul in His hands?" I conjure thee by the
living God do it, man, and thy soul is saved. Oh,
by Him who from the highest throne in glory stooped
to the Cross of deepest ignominy, trust thy soul with
Him. It is all He asks of thee, and this He gives thee.

Blessed Master, would that Thou couldst stand
here, and say, "Sinners, full of iniquity, I stood with
you; God accounted Me as if I had committed *your sin*,
and visited Me as if I had been a transgressor; trust
Me; cast your souls upon My perfect righteousness;

wash in My cleansing Blood, and I will make you whole, and present you faultless before My Father's face. "

II. We are taught in the next sentence, that Christ

"Bare the Sins of Many."

Here it is as clear as noonday, that Christ dealt with **sinners**. Do not say Christ died for those who have done no wrong. That is not the description given. It is clear, I say, to every one that chooses to look, that Christ could not bear the sins of those who had no sins, but could only bear the sins of men who were sinful and guilty. Briefly, then, but very plainly, to recount the old, old story over again: man stood with a load of sin upon his shoulders, so heavy that it would have crushed him lower than the lowest Hell; Christ Jesus came into the world, stood in the room, place, and stead of His people; and He did, in the expressive words of the text, *bear their sins* —that is to say, their sins were really, not in a legal fiction, but really transferred from them to Him.

You see, a man cannot bear a thing which is not on his back; it is impossible that he can bear it unless it is actually there. The word "bear" implies weight, and weight is the sure indicator of reality. Christ did bear sin in its fulness, vileness, and condemnation upon His own shoulders. Comprehend this, then, and you have the marrow of the subject. Christ did really, literally, and truly, take the sins that belonged to all who do believe on Him, and those sins did actually and in very deed become His sins (not that He had committed them, nor that He had any part or lot in them, except through the imputation to which He had consented, and for which He came into the world), and there lay the sins of all His people upon Christ's shoulders.

2. Then notice, that as He did bear them, so other texts tell us that **He did bear them away.** "Behold the Lamb of God, which taketh away the sin of the world." Sin being on His head, the scape-goat took it away, away, away. Where? Into the wilderness of forgetfulness. If it be sought for it shall not be found; the Everlasting God seeth it no more, it hath ceased to be, for He hath finished iniquity and made an end of sin; and when there is an end of it what more can be said?

3. And then you must understand that if it be so, if Christ did really bear His people's sins, and did bear them away—and since a thing cannot be in two places at one time, **there is now no sin abiding**

upon those for whom Jesus died. "And who are they?" you say. Why, all those who trust Him. Any man whatsoever, the wide world over, who shall ever trust Christ, may know that no sin can be with him because his sin was laid on Christ. Oh, I do delight in this precious doctrine! If anything could unloose my poor stammering tongue, this might, to see sin literally transferred so that there is none left! I cannot express the delight and joy of my soul at this moment, in contemplation of the blessed deliverance and release which Christ has given. I can only sing out again with Kent:

> "Sons of God, redeemed by blood,
> Raise your songs to Zion's God—
> Made from condemnation free,
> Grace triumphant sing with me."

It is as sinners, not as sensible sinners, not as repenting sinners, that Jesus died for us. Sinners as sinners, Jesus Christ has chosen, redeemed, and called; in fact, for them, and for only such, Jesus Christ came into the world.

III. Our third sentence tells us that

Jesus Intercedes for Sinners.

"AND MADE INTERCESSION FOR THE TRANSGRESSORS."

He prays for His saints, but, dear friends, remember

that by nature they are transgressors, and nothing more. What does our text say? He intercedes for transgressors! There is a transgressor here. He has been hearing the Gospel for many years; and he has heard it preached faithfully, too. He is growing grey now; but while his head is getting white his heart is black; he is an old hard-hearted reprobate, and by and by, unless grace prevents——but I need not tell that story. What is that I hear? The feet of justice, slowly but surely coming. I hear a voice saying: "Lo, these three years I come seeking fruit on this fig tree and find none; cut it down; why cumbereth it the ground?" (Luke 13. 7). The woodman feels his axe; it is sharp and keen. "Now," says he, "I will lay to at this barren tree, and cut it down." But, hark! There is one that maketh intercession for transgressors, hear Him, hear Him, "Spare it yet a little while, till I dig about it and dung it, and if it bear fruit *well*; but if not, after that thou shalt cut it down."

You see there was nothing in that tree why he should plead for it, and there is nothing in you why He should plead for you, yet He does it. This very day, perhaps, He is crying, "Spare him yet a little while; let him hear the Gospel again; let him

be entreated once more; oh! let him have another
sickness that it may make his conscience feel; let Me
have another endeavour with his hard heart; it may
be, it may be that he will yield." O sinner, bless
God that Jesus Christ pleads for you in that way.

But that done, **He pleads for their forgiveness.**
They are nailing Him to the Cross; the wretches are
driving iron through His hands; but even while they
fasten Him to the tree hear Him: "Father, forgive
them, for they know not what they do." Oh, I spoke
to a brother this week, whose heart all-conquering
love has touched. He had been a great blasphemer,
and when we were talking together about the fact that
Jesus Christ loved him even when he was cursing, I
saw how it broke His heart; and it broke mine too, to
think that I could rebel against Christ while He was
loving me; that I could despise Him while He was
putting Himself in my way in order to do me good.

There is a man there who has been cursing, and
swearing, and blaspheming, and the very Man whom
he has cursed has been crying, "Father, forgive him,
for he knows not what he does." O sinner, I would
that this might break thy heart, and bring thee to
the Saviour.

There are a great many sermons preached that have

not the Gospel in them, especially those sermons the
drift of which is to tell the sinners, "Go home and
pray." That is very good advice, but it is not the
Gospel. The sinner might answer me, "How can I
come before God as I am; I cannot plead before Him,
for I am a wretch undone; if I should stand in His
presence He would drive me from Him." Behold
Jesus Christ maketh intercession for transgressors.
It is a common saying in the world, that a man who
pleads his own cause has a fool for his client, certainly
it is so in Heaven. But when Christ comes in, the
Wonderful, the Counsellor, He takes up the brief, and
now the adversary trembles, for no sooner does he find
that the suit is put into the hands of Him who is the
Advocate of His people than he knows that his case
is lost, and that the sinner will go free.

I come to a conclusion reluctantly; but I must say
these few words. There are some of you that make
very light of sinning. I pray you be reasonable, and
think this matter over. It was no light thing for God
to save a sinner, for the Son of God Himself must be
numbered with sinners, and smart and die for sinners,
or else they could not be saved.

To you who make but little of Christ, there is this
word: you know what sin means; I do not think you

can ever make too *much* of sin, but I pray you do not make too *little* of Christ. To you who think you have no qualifications for Christ, I say this closing sentence: I do beseech you get rid of that foul, that legal, that soul-destroying idea that *Christ wants any preparation by you* or in you before you come to Him. You may come to Him now; nay, more, **you are commanded to come to Him** now, just as you are. And to every man among you to-day, and to every woman and child, I preach this Gospel in the Name of Jesus Christ: "Believe on the Lord Jesus Christ, and thou shalt be saved." Trust Him now—in your seat—standing in the aisles—crowded in these galleries—trust Him now; God commands you. "This is *the* commandment, that ye believe on Jesus Christ whom He hath sent" (John 6. 29). As Peter said, so say I, Repent and be converted, every one of you (Acts 3. 19); and as Paul said to the Philippian jailer, so say I, "Believe on the Lord Jesus Christ, and thou shalt be saved, and thy house" (Acts 16. 31). Can you do it? Can you trust Him *now*? Is it a full trust? Are you leaning on your feelings? Give them up. Are you depending a little on what you mean to do? Give that up. Do you trust Him wholly? Can you say, "His blessed wounds, His flowing Blood,

His perfect righteousness, on these I rest. I do trust Him wholly?" Are you half afraid to say you do? Do you think it is such a bold thing? Do it then; do a bold thing for once! Say, "Lord, I'll trust Thee, and if Thou cast me away, I'll still trust Thee; I bless Thee that Thou canst save me, and that Thou wilt save me."

But I hear one say, "It is too good to be true!" Soul, wilt thou be lost through thinking little things of Christ? "Ah!" says another, "it is too simple; if this be the Gospel, we shall have all the ragamuffins in the streets believing in Christ and being saved." And glory be to God if it be so! For my part I am never afraid of big sinners being saved. I would have every harlot, I would have every adulterer to be saved. I would not be afraid that they would go on in their sins if they believed in Christ. Oh! no; faith in Christ would change their nature; and it will change yours too; for this is salvation: to have the nature changed, to be made a new creature in Christ, and to be made holy.

Come as you are. If you are the blackest soul out of Hell, trust Christ, and that act of trust shall make you clean. This seems a simple thing, and yet it is the hardest thing in the world to bring you to it; so

4

hard a thing that all the preachers that ever preached cannot make a man believe in Christ. Though we put it as plainly as we can, and plead with you, you only go away and say, "It is too good to be true;" or else you despise it because it is so simple; for the Gospel, like Christ, is despised and rejected of men, because it has no form and comeliness, and no beauty in it that they should desire it. Oh! may the Holy Ghost lay this home to you; may He make you willing in the day of His power. I hope He has; I trust He has, so that ere we part we may join in singing this verse:

> "A guilty, weak, and helpless worm,
>   On Christ's kind arms I fall;
> He is my strength, my righteousness,
>   My Jesus, and my all."

The King's Highway Opened and Cleared

"And they said, Believe on the Lord Jesus Christ and thou shalt be saved, and thy house" (Acts 16. 31).

WHEN the children of Israel were settled in Canaan, God ordained that they should set apart certain cities to be called the Cities of Refuge, that to these the man-slayer might flee for security. If he killed another unawares, and had no malice aforethought, he might flee at once to the City of Refuge; and if he could enter its gates before the avenger of blood should overtake him, he would be secure. We are told by the rabbis that once in the year, or oftener, the magistrates of the district were accustomed to survey the high roads which led to these cities: they carefully gathered up all the stones, and took the greatest possible precautions that there should be no stumbling-blocks in the way which might cause the poor fugitives to fall, or might by any means impede him in his hasty course. We hear, moreover, and we believe the tradition to be grounded in fact, that all

along the road there were hand-posts with the words
"Refuge" written very legibly upon them; so that
when the fugitive came to a cross-road, he might not
need to question for a single moment which was the
way of escape; but seeing the well-known word
"Refuge, " he kept on his breathless and headlong
course until he had entered the suburb of the City
of Refuge, and he was then at once completely safe.

God has prepared for the sons of men a City of
Refuge, and the way to it is by FAITH IN CHRIST JESUS.
I propose to go along the road, and, by God's grace,
to remove any impediment which Satan may have laid
upon the path.

I have thus given the reasons why I am compelled in
spirit to make this survey this morning.

The road to Heaven, my brethren, is

By Faith in Christ Jesus.

It is not by well-doing that you can be saved, though
it is by ill-doing that you will be damned if you put
not trust in Christ. Nothing that you can do can save
you. Albeit that after you are saved it will be your
delightful privilege to walk in the ways of God and to
keep His commandments, yet all your own attempts
to keep the commandments previous to faith will but

sink you deeper into the mire, and will by no means contribute to your salvation. The one road to Heaven is *by Faith in Christ.* Or to make it plainer still, as the countryman said, there are but two steps to Heaven—out of self into Christ; and, then, out of Christ into Heaven. Faith is simply explained as *trusting in Christ.* I find that Christ commands me to believe in Him, or to trust Him. I feel that there is no reason in myself why I should be allowed to trust Him. But He *commands* me to do so. Therefore, altogether apart from my character or from any preparation that I feel in myself, I obey the command, and sink or swim, I trust Christ. The leaving of the soul in the hands of Jesus is the very essence of faith. Faith is receiving Christ with the understanding and with the will, submitting everything to Him, taking Him to be my all in all, and agreeing to be henceforth nothing at all. Faith is ceasing from the creature and coming to the Creator. It is looking out of self to Christ, turning the eye entirely from any good thing that is here within me, and looking for every blessing to those open veins, to that poor bleeding Heart, to that thorn-crowned Head, of Him whom God hath set forth "to be the propitiation for our sins, and not for our sins only, but for the sins of the whole world. "

Well, having thus described the way, I now come to my real business of removing these stones:

I. A very common impediment in the pathway of the soul that is desiring to be saved is

The Recollection of its Past Life.

"Oh," saith the sinner, "I dare not trust Christ, because my past sins have been of an unusually black dye. I have been no common sinner, but I have been one singled out from the herd, a very monster in sin. I have taken the highest degree in the devil's college, and have become a master of Belial. I have learned to sit in the seat of the scornful, and have taught others to rebel against God." You recollect how you have cursed God, and you say, "Can I, dare I trust Him whom I have cursed?" And your old lusts are now rising before you; midnight sins stare you in the face, and snatches of the lascivious song are being yelled in the ear of your poor convinced conscience. And all your sins as they rise up, cry, "Depart, thou accursed one! Depart! thou hast sinned thyself out of grace! Thou art a condemned one! Depart! There is no hope, there is no mercy for thee!"

Now, permit me in the strength and Name of God to remove this stumbling-block out of your way.

Sinner, I tell thee that all thy sins, be they never so many, cannot destroy thee if thou dost believe on the Lord Jesus Christ. If now thou castest thyself simply on the merits of Jesus, "Though thy sins be as scarlet, they shall be as wool." *"Only believe."* Dare to believe that Christ is able to save them to the uttermost that come unto God by Him. Take Him at His word and trust Him. And thou hast a warrant for doing it; for remember it is written, "The Blood of Jesus Christ, His Son, cleanseth us from *all sin*." If thy sins were ten thousand times as many as they be, yet the Blood of Christ is able to atone for them all. Only dare to believe that. Now, but a venturesome faith, trust thyself to Christ. If thou obey God in this matter of putting thy trust in Christ, God's own Word is guaranteed that thy faith shall be rewarded, and thou shalt find that thy sins which are many are all forgiven thee. By the side of Saul of Tarsus, and of her out of whom was cast seven devils, shalt thou one day stand. With the thief shalt thou sing of love Divine, and with Manasseh shalt thou rejoice in Him who can wash away the foulest crimes. Oh, I pray God there may be some one in this great crowd to-day who may be saying in his heart, "Sir, you have described *me*. I do feel that I am the blackest sinner anywhere, but

I will risk it, I will put my trust in Christ and Christ
alone." If thou canst do this I will be God's hostage
that He will be true to thee and true to His Son, for
never sinner perished yet that dared to trust the precious Blood of Christ.

Now let me endeavour to upheave and eject another
stumblingblock:

II. "Oh," saith some poor soul, "I do not know
whether I believe or not, sir. Sometimes I do believe;
but, oh,

It is Such a Little Faith I Have

that I cannot think Christ can save me." Ah, there
you are again, you see, looking to yourself. This
has made many trip and fall. I pray God I may put
this out of your way. Poor sinner, remember it is not
the *strength* of thy faith that saves thee, but the *reality*
of thy faith. What is more, it is not even the reality
of thy faith that saves thee, it is the *object* of thy faith.
If thy faith be fixed on Christ, though it seems to be
in itself a line no thicker than a spider's cobweb, it
will hold thy soul throughout time and eternity. For
remember it is not the thickness of this cable of faith,
it is the strength of the anchor which imparts strength
to the cable, and so shall hold thy ship in the midst
of the most fearful storm. The faith that saves man

is sometimes so small that the man himself cannot see it. A grain of mustard seed is the smallest of all seeds, and yet if thou hast but that quantity of faith, thou art a saved man.

Remember what the poor woman did. She did not come and take hold of Christ's person with her hands, she did not throw her arms about his knees; but she stretched out her finger, and then—she did not touch Christ's feet or even his dress—she touched but the ravelling, the *fringe* of His garment, and she was made whole. If thy faith be but as little as that, seek to get more of it, but still remember that it will save thee. Remember a little child belongs to the human race as much as the greatest giant; and so a babe in grace is as truly a child of God as is Mr. Great-heart, who can fight all the giants on the road. And thou mayest be as much an heir of Heaven in thy minority, in the infancy of thy grace, as thou wilt be when thou shalt have expanded into the full grown Christian, and shalt become a perfect man in Christ Jesus. It is not, I tell thee, the *strength of thy faith*, but *the object* of thy faith. It is the blood, not the hyssop; not the hand that smites the lintel, but the blood that secures the Israelite in the day when God's vengeance passes by. Let that stumbling-block be taken away.

III. "But," saith another, "I do think sometimes I have a little faith, but

I have so many Doubts and Fears.

I am tempted every day to believe that Jesus Christ did not die for me, or that my belief is not genuine, or that I never experienced the regenerating influence of the Holy Spirit. Tell me, sir, can I be a true believer in Christ if I have doubts and fears?" My answer is simply this, there is no Scripture which saith, that "He that believeth shall be damned, if that faith be mixed with doubts." "He that believeth shall be saved," be that faith never so little, and even though it be intermingled with multitudes of doubts and fears.

You remember that memorable story of our Saviour, when He was on board a ship with His disciples. The winds roared, the ship rocked to and fro, the mast was strained, the sails were rent, and the poor disciples were full of fear: "Lord, save us, or we perish." Here were doubts. What did Jesus say when he rebuked them? "Why are ye fearful"—O ye of *no* faith? No; "O ye of *little* faith." So there may be little faith where there are great doubts.

Do you not know that the best of God's children are

exercised with doubts and fears even to the last? Look at such a man as John Knox. There was a man who could face the frowns of a world, who could speak like a king to kings, and fear no man; yet on his dying bed he was troubled about his interest in Christ, because he was tempted to self-righteousness. If such a man have doubts, dost *thou* expect to live without them? If God's brightest saints are exercised, if Paul himself keeps under his body lest he should be a castaway, why, how canst thou expect to live without clouds? Oh, my dear man, drop the idea that the prevalence of thy doubts disproves the truth of the promise. Again believe; away with all thy doubts; sink or swim, cast thyself on Jesus; and thou canst not be lost, for His honour is engaged to save every soul that puts its trust in Him.

IV. "Ah," says another, "but you have not yet hit upon my fear." I used when I first knew the Saviour, to try myself in a certain manner, and often did I throw stumbling-blocks in my path through it, and therefore I can speak very affectionately to any of you who are doing the same. Sometimes I would go up into my chamber, and by way of self-examination, say to myself:

I am Afraid to Die.

If I should drop down dead in my chamber, can I say that I should joyfully close my eyes? Well, it often happened that I could not honestly say so. I used to feel that death would be a very solemn thing. Ah, then, I said, "I have never believed in Christ, for if I had put my trust in the Lord Jesus, I should not be afraid to die, but I should be quite confident." I do not doubt that there are many here who are saying, "Sir, I cannot follow Christ, because I am afraid to die; I cannot believe that Jesus Christ will save me, because the sight of death makes me tremble." I remember my aged grandfather once preach a sermon which I have not forgotten. He was preaching from the text, "The God of all grace," and he somewhat interested the assembly, after describing the different kinds of grace that God gave, by saying at the end of each period, "But there is one kind of grace that you do not want." After each sentence there came the like, "But there is one kind of grace you do not want." And, then, he wound up by saying, "You don't want dying grace in living moments, but you shall have dying grace when you want it." Do not expect dying grace until you want it, and when the time comes, you may be sure you will have sufficient grace to bear it. Cast out that stumbling-block then. Rest thyself on Christ, and trust a living Christ to help thee in thy dying hour.

V. Another most grievous perplexity to many a seeking soul is this: "Oh, I would trust Christ, but

I Feel No Joy.

I hear the children of God singing sweetly about their privileges, I hear them saying that they have been to the top of Pisgah and have viewed the promised land, have taken a pleasant prospect of the world to come; but, oh, my faith yields me no joy. I hope I do believe, but at the same time I have none of those raptures. My worldly troubles press heavily upon me, and sometimes even my spiritual woes are greater than I can bear." Ah, poor soul, let me cast out that stone from thy road. Remember, it is not written, "He that is joyful shall be saved," but "He that *believeth* shall be saved." Thy faith will make thee joyful by and by; but it is as powerful to save thee even when it does not make thee rejoice. Why, look at many of God's people, how sad and sorrowful they have been! I know they ought not to be. This is their sin; but still it is such a sin that it does not destroy the efficacy of faith. Notwithstanding all the sorrows of the saints, faith still keeps alive, and God is still true to His promise. Remember, it is not what you feel that saves you; it is what you believe. It is not feeling, but believing. "We walk by *faith*, not by sight" (2 Cor. 5. 7). When I feel my soul as cold as an iceberg, as hard as a rock, and as sinful as Satan, yet even then faith ceases not to justify. Faith prevails as truly in the midst of sad feelings as of happy feelings, for then, standing alone, it proves the majesty of its might. Believe, O son of God, believe in Him, and look not for aught in thyself.

VI. Then, again, there are many that are distressed because

They have Blasphemous Thoughts.

Here, too, I can heartily sympathise with many. I remember a certain narrow and crooked lane in a certain country town, along which I was walking one day while I was seeking the Saviour. On a sudden the most fearful oaths that any of you can conceive rushed through my heart. I put my hand to my mouth to prevent the utterance. I had not, that I know of, ever heard those words; and I am certain that I had never used in my life from my youth up so much as one of them, for I had never been profane. But these things sorely beset me; for half an hour together the most fearful imprecations would dash through my brain. Oh, how I groaned and cried before God! That temptation passed away; but ere many days it was renewed again; and when I was in prayer, or when I was reading the Bible, these blasphemous thoughts would pour in upon me more than at any other time. I consulted with an aged godly man about it. He said to me, "Oh, all this many of the people of God have proved before you. But," said he, "do you hate these thoughts?" "I do," I truly said. "Then," said he, "they are not yours; serve them as the old parishes used to do with vagrants—whip them and send them on to their own parish. So," said he, "do with them. Groan over them, repent of them, and sent them on to the Devil, the father of them, to whom they belong—for they are not yours."

Now, come, poor soul, notwithstanding all these blasphemous thoughts in thy soul, dare to put thy trust in Christ. Even should those thoughts have been more blasphemous than any thou hast ever heard, come trust in Christ, come cast thyself on Him. I have heard that when an elephant is going over a bridge he will sound the timber with his foot to see if it will bear him over. Come thou, who thinkest thyself an elephantine sinner, here is a bridge that is strong enough for thee, even with all these thoughts of thine: "All manner of sin and blasphemy shall be forgiven thee." Throw that in Satan's face, and trust thyself to Christ.

VII. One other stumbling-block, and I will have done. Some there be that say, "Oh, sir, I would trust in Christ to save me

If I could see that my Faith Brought forth Fruits. Oh, sir, when I would do good, evil is present with me." Excuse my always bringing in my own feelings as an illustration, but I feel when I am preaching to tried sinners, that the testimony of one's own experience is generally more powerful than any other illustration that can be found. It is not, believe me, any display of egotism, but the simple desire to come home to you, that makes me state what I have felt myself. The first Sunday after I came to Christ, I went to a Methodist chapel. The sermon was upon this text: "O wretched man that I am! who shall deliver me from the body of this death?" I had just got as far as that in the week. I knew that I had put my trust in Christ, and I knew that, when I sat in that house of prayer, my faith was simply and solely fixed on the atonement of the Redeemer. But I had a weight

on my mind, because I could not be as holy as I wanted
to be. I could not live without sin. When I rose in
the morning I thought I would abstain from every
hard word, from every evil thought and look; and I
came up to that chapel groaning, because "when I
would do good evil was present with me." I know
that Paul was a Christian, and I know the more
Christians look to themselves the more they will have
to groan, because they cannot be what they want to be.

What, you will not believe in Christ until you are
perfect? Then you will never believe in Him. You
will not trust the precious Jesus till you have no sins
to trust Him with! Then you will never trust Him
at all. I know one man who thought himself a perfect
man, and that man was hump-backed. This was my
rebuke to his pride, "Surely if the Lord gave you a
perfect soul he would give you a perfect body to carry
it in." Perfection will not be found this side of the
grave. Your business is to trust in Christ. You must
depend on nothing but the Blood of Christ. Trust in
Christ and you stand secure. "He that believeth on
the Son of God hath everlasting life."

I would lay this road as straight and clear as ever
was turnpike road between one city and another.
Sinner, there is nothing which can rob thee of *thy right*

5

to believe in Christ. Thou art freely invited to come
to the marriage banquet. The table is spread, and
the invitation is freely given. There are no porters
at the door to keep thee out; there are none to ask a
ticket of admission of thee:

> "Let not conscience make you linger;
> Nor of fitness fondly dream;
> All the fitness He requireth
> Is to feel your need of Him;
> *This He gives you*:
> 'Tis His Spirit's rising beam."

And I would again, even to the falling down on my
knees, as though God did beseech you by me, "pray
you in Christ's stead, be ye reconciled to God"
(2 Cor. 5. 20).   And this is the reconciliation,
"That ye believe on the Lord Jesus Christ whom He
hath sent," that ye trust Christ. Do you understand
me? That ye cast yourself on Him; that ye depend on
nothing but what He has done. Saved you must be,
lost you cannot be, if you fling yourself wholly upon
Christ, and cast the whole burden of your sins, your
doubts, your fears, and your anxieties wholly there.

Christ—Our Substitute

"For He hath made Him to be sin for us, who knew no sin; that we might be made the righteousness of God in Him" (2 Cor. 5. 21).

SOME time ago an excellent lady sought an interview with me, with the object as she said, of enlisting my sympathy upon the question of "Anti-Capital Punishment." I heard the excellent reasons she urged against hanging men who committed murder, and though they did not convince me, I did not seek to answer them. She proposed that when a man committed murder, he should be confined for life. My remark was, that a great many men who had been confined half their lives were not a bit the better for it, and as for her belief that they would necessarily be brought to repentance, I was afraid it was but a dream. "Ah," she said, good soul as she was, "that is because we have been all wrong about punishments. We punish people because we think they deserve to be punished. Now, we ought to show them," said she, "that we love them; that we only punish them to make them better." "Indeed, madam," I said, "I have heard that theory a great many times, and I have seen much fine writing upon the matter, but I am no believer in it. The design of punishment should be amendment, but the ground of punishment lies in the positive guilt of the offender. I believe that when a man does wrong, he ought to be punished for it, and that there is a guilt in sin which justly merits punishment." "Oh no; she could not see that. Sin was a very wrong thing, but punishment was not a proper idea. She thought that people were treated too cruelly in prison, and that they ought to be taught that we love them. If they were treated kindly in prison, and tenderly dealt with, they would grow so much better, she was sure."

With a view of interpreting her own theory, I said, I suppose, then, you would give criminals all sorts of indulgences in prison. Some great vagabond who has committed burglary dozens of times—I suppose you would let him sit in an easy chair in the evening before a nice fire, and mix him a glass of spirits and water, and give him his pipe, and make him happy, to show how much we love him." "Well, no, she would not give him the spirits, but, still, all the rest would do him good."

I thought that was a delightful picture certainly.

It seemed to me to be the most prolific method of cultivating rogues which ingenuity could invent. I imagine that you could grow any number of thieves in that way; for it would be a special means of propagating all manner of roguery and wickedness. These very delightful theories to such a simple mind as mine, were the source of much amusement, the idea of fondling villains, and treating their crimes as if they were the tumbles and falls of children, made me laugh heartily. I fancied I saw the government resigning its functions to these excellent persons, and the grand results of their marvellously kind experiments. The sword of the magistrate transformed into a gruel-spoon, and the jail become a sweet retreat for injured reputations.

Little, however, did I think I should live to see this kind of stuff taught in pulpits; I had no idea that there would come out a divinity, which would bring down God's moral government from the solemn aspect in which Scripture reveals it, to a namby-pamby sentimentalism, which adores a Deity destitute of every masculine virtue. But we never know to-day what may occur to-morrow. We have lived to see a certain sort of men, who seek to teach now-a-days, that God is a universal Father, and that our ideas of

His dealing with the impenitent as a Judge, and not as a Father, are remnants of antiquated error. Sin, according to these men, is a disorder rather than an offence, an error rather than a crime. Love is the only attribute they can discern, and the full-orbed Deity they have not known. Some of these men push their way very far into the bogs and mire of false-hood, until they inform us that eternal punishment is ridiculed as a dream. In fact, books now appear, which teach us that there is no such thing as the Vicarious Sacrifice of our Lord Jesus Christ. They use the word Atonement, it is true, but in regard to its meaning they have removed the ancient landmark. They acknowledge that the Father has shown His great love to poor sinful man by sending His Son, but not that God was inflexibly just in the exhibition of His mercy, not that He punished Christ on the behalf of His people, nor that indeed God ever will punish any-body in His wrath, or that there is such a thing as justice apart from discipline. Even *sin* and *Hell* are but old words employed henceforth in a new and altered sense.

Well, I come to address you upon the topic which is most continually assailed by those who preach another Gospel "which is not another"—but there be some that trouble you, and would pervert the Gospel of Christ," namely, the doctrine of the substitution of Christ on our behalf, His actual atonement for our sins, and our positive and actual justification through His sufferings and righteousness. It seems to me that until language can mean the very reverse of what it says, until by some strange logic, God's Word can be contradicted and can be made to belie itself, the doctrine of *substitution* can never be rooted out of the words which I have selected for my text, "He hath made Him to be sin for us, who knew no sin, that we might be made the righteousness of God in Him."

I. First,

The Sinlessness of the Substitute."

"WHO KNEW NO SIN." The doctrine of Holy Scripture is this, that inasmuch as man could not keep God's law, having fallen in Adam, Christ came and suffered in the room, place, and stead of His elect ones, that so by His enduring the full vials of wrath, they might be emptied out and not a drop might ever fall upon the heads of His blood-bought people. Now, you will readily perceive that if one is to be a substitute for another before God, either to work out a righteousness or to suffer a penalty, that substitute must Himself be free from sin. If he hath sin of his own, all that he can suffer will but be the due reward of his own iniquity. If he hath himself transgressed, he cannot suffer for another, because all his sufferings are already due on his own personal account.

1. It is satisfactory for us to know, and to believe beyond a doubt, that **our Lord Jesus was without sin**. Of course, in His Divine nature He could not know iniquity; and as for His human nature, it never knew the original taint of depravity. He was of the seed of the woman, but not of the tainted and infected seed of Adam. Overshadowed as was the Virgin by the Holy Ghost, no corruption entered into His nativity. That holy thing which was born of her was neither conceived in sin nor shapen in iniquity. He was brought into this world immaculate. He was immaculately conceived and immaculately born. In Him that natural black blood which we have inherited from Adam never dwelt. His heart was upright within Him; His soul was without any bias to evil; His imagination had never been darkened. He had no infatuated mind. There was no tendency whatever in Him but to do that which was good, holy, and honourable. And as He did not share in the original depravity, so He did not share in the

imputed sin of Adam which we have inherited—not,
I mean, in Himself personally, though He took the
consequences of that, as He stood as our representative.
The sin of Adam had never passed over the head of
the Second Adam. All that were in the loins of Adam
sinned in him when he touched the fruit; but Jesus
was not in the loins of Adam. Though He might be
conceived of as being in the womb of the woman—
"a new thing which the Lord created in the earth"—
He lay not in Adam when he sinned, and consequently
no guilt from Adam, either of depravity of nature, or
of distance from God, ever fell upon Jesus as the result
of anything that Adam did. I mean upon Jesus as
considered *in Himself* though He certainly took the
sin of Adam as He was the representative of His
people.

2. Again, as in His nature He was free from the
corruption and condemnation of the sin of Adam, so
also in His life, no sin ever corrupted His way. **He
did no sin**. His eye never flashed with unhallowed
anger; His lip never uttered a treacherous or deceitful
word; His heart never harboured an evil imagination.
Never did He wander after lust; no covetousness ever
so much as glanced into His soul. He was "holy,
harmless, undefiled, separate from sinners." From

the beginning of His life to the end, you cannot put your finger even upon a mistake, much less upon a wilful error.

So perfect was He, that no virtue seemed to preponderate, or by an opposing quality give a bias to the scale of absolute rectitude.   John is distinguished for his love, Peter for his courage; but Jesus Christ is distinguished for neither one above another, because He possessed all in such sublime unison, such Heavenly harmony, that no one virtue stands out above the rest. He is meek, but He is courageous.   He is loving, but He is decided; He is bold as a lion, yet He is quiet and peaceful as a lamb.   He was like that fine flour which was offered before God in the burnt offering; a flour without grit, so smooth, that when you rubbed it, it was soft and pure, no particles could be discerned: so was His character fully ground, fully compounded.

There was not one feature in His moral countenance which had undue preponderance above the other; but He was replete in everything that was virtuous and good.   Tempted He was, it is true, but sinned He never.

Never once did He even seem to bend before the tempest; but buffetting the fury of the blast, bearing all the temptations that could ever happen to man,

which summed themselves up and consummated their
fury on Him, He stood to the end, without a single
flaw in His life, or a stain upon His spotless robe.
Let us rejoice, then, in this, that we have *such a
Substitute*—one who is fit and proper to stand in our
place, and to suffer in your stead, seeing He has no
need to offer a sacrifice for Himself; no need to cry for
Himself, "Father, I have sinned;" no need to bend
the knee of the penitent and confess His own iniquities,
for He is without spot or blemish, the perfect Lamb of
God's passover.

3. I would have you carefully notice the particular
expression of the text, for it struck me as being very
beautiful and significant—"Who knew no sin." It
does not merely say *did* none, but *knew* none. Sin was
no acquaintance of His; He was acquainted with grief,
but no acquaintance of sin. He had to walk in the
midst of its most frequented haunts, but did not know
it; not that He was ignorant of its nature or did not
know its penalty, but He did not *know it*; He was a
stranger to it. Of course He knew what sin was, for
He was very God, but with sin He had no commun on,
no fellowship, no brotherhood. He was a perfect
stranger in the presence of sin; He was a foreigner; He
was not an inhabitant of that land where sin is acknow-

ledged. He passed through the wilderness of suffering,
but into the wilderness of sin He could never go.

"He *knew* no sin;" mark that expression and treasure it up, and when you are thinking of your substitute, and see Him hang bleeding upon the Cross,
think that you see written in these lines of blood
written along His blessed body, "He *knew* no sin."
Mingled with the redness of His Blood—that Rose of
Sharon; behold the purity of His nature, the Lily of
the Valley—"He *knew* no sin."

II. Let us pass on to notice the second and most
important point;

The Actual Substitution of Christ,

AND THE REAL IMPUTATION OF SIN TO HIM.   "HE
MADE HIM TO BE SIN FOR US."

1. Here be careful to observe **who transferred the
sin**. God the Father laid on Jesus the iniquities of
us all. Man could not make Christ sin. Man could
not transfer His guilt to another. It is not for us to
say whether Christ could or could not have made
Himself sin for us; but certain it is, He did not take
this priesthood upon Himself, but He was *called of
God*, as was Aaron. The Redeemer's vicarious
position is warranted, nay ordained by Divine

authority. "HE hath made Him to be sin for us."

I must now beg you to notice how very explicit the term is. Some of our expositors will have it that the word here used must mean "sin-offering." "He made Him to be a sin-offering for us." I thought it well to look to my Greek Testament to see whether it could be so. Of course we all know that the word here translated "sin," is very often translated "sin-offering," but it is always useful, when you have a disputed passage, to look it through, and see whether in this case the word would bear such a meaning. These commentators say it means a sin-offering. Well, I will read it: "He hath made Him to be a sin-offering for us who knew no *sin-offering*." Does not that strike you as being ridiculous? But they are precisely the same words; and if it be fair to translate it "sin-offering" in one place, it must, in all reason, be fair to translate it so in the other. The fact is, while in some passages it may be rendered "sin-offering," in this passage it cannot be so, because it would be to run counter to all honesty to translate the same word in the same sentence two different ways. No; we must take them as they stand. "He hath made Him to be sin for us," not merely an offering, but *sin* for us.

MARTIN LUTHER is reputed to have broadly said that although Jesus Christ was sinless, yet He was the greatest sinner that ever lived, because all the sins of His people lay upon Him. Now, such expressions I think to be unguarded, if not profane. The fact is, that in no sense whatever—take that as I say it—in no sense whatever can Jesus Christ ever be conceived of as having been guilty. *"He knew no sin."* Not only was He not guilty of any sin which He committed Himself, but He was not guilty of our sins. No guilt can possibly attach to a man who has not been guilty. He must have had complicity in the deed itself, or else no *guilt* can possibly be laid on Him. Jesus Christ stands in the midst of all the Divine thunders, and suffers all the punishment, but not a drop of sin ever stained Him. In no sense is He ever a guilty man, but always is He an accepted and a holy one.

What, then, is the meaning of that very forcible expression of my text? We must interpret Scriptural modes of expression by the verbiage of the speakers. We know that our Master once said Himself, "This cup is the new covenant in My Blood;" He did not mean that the cup was the covenant. He said, "Take, eat, this is My Body"—no one of us conceives that the bread is the literal flesh and Blood of Christ. We take that bread as if it were the body, and it actually represents it. Now, we are to read a passage like this, according to the analogy of faith. Jesus Christ was made by His Father sin for us; that is, He was treated as if He had Himself been sin. He was not sin; He was not sinful; He was not guilty; but, *He was treated by His Father, as if He had not only been sinful, but as if he had been sin itself*. That is a strong expression used here.

2. Not only hath He made Him to be the substitute for sin, but **to be sin**. God looked on Christ as if Christ had been sin; not as if He had taken up the sins of His people, or as if they were laid on Him, though that were true, but as if He Himself had positively been that noxious—that God-hating—that soul-damning thing, called sin. When the Judge of all the earth said, "Where is Sin?" Christ presented Himself. He stood before His Father as if He had been the accumulation of all human guilt; as if He Himself were that thing which God cannot endure, but which He must drive from His presence for ever.

And now see how this making of Jesus to be sin was enacted to the fullest extent. The righteous Lord looked on Christ as being sin, and therefore Christ must be taken without the camp. Sin cannot be borne in God's Zion, cannot be allowed to dwell in God's Jerusalem; it must be taken without the camp, it is a leprous thing, put it away. Cast out from fellowship, from love, from pity, sin must ever be. Take Him away, take Him away, ye crowd! Hurry Him through the streets and bear Him to Calvary. Take Him without the camp—as was the beast which was offered for sin without the camp, so must Christ be, who was made sin for us.

And now, God looks on Him as being sin, and sin must bear punishment. Christ is punished. The most fearful of deaths is exacted at His hand, and God has no pity for Him. How shall he have pity on sin? God hates it. No tongue can tell, no soul can divine the terrible hatred of God to that which is evil, and He treats Christ as if He were sin. He prays, but Heaven shuts out His prayer; He cries for water, but Heaven and earth refuse to wet His lips except with vinegar. He turns His eye to Heaven, He sees nothing there. How should He? God cannot look on sin, and sin can have no claim on God: "My God, My God," He cries, "why hast Thou forsaken Me?"

O solemn necessity, how could God do anything with sin but forsake it? How could iniquity have fellowship with God? Shall Divine smiles rest on sin? Nay, nay, it must not be. Therefore is it that He who is made sin must bemoan desertion and terror. God cannot touch Him, cannot dwell with Him, cannot come near Him. He is abhorred, cast away; it hath pleased the Father to bruise Him; He hath put him to grief.

I do not know whether I have clearly uttered what I want to state, but what a grim picture that is, to conceive of sin gathered up into one mass—murder, lust and rapine, and adultery, and all manner of crime, all piled together in one hideous heap. We ourselves, impure though we be, could not bear this; how much less should God with His pure and holy eyes bear with that mass of sin, and yet there it is, and God looked upon Christ as if He were that mass of sin. He was not sin, but He looked upon Him as made sin for us. He stands in our place, assumes our guilt, takes on Him our iniquity, and God treats Him as if He had been sin.

3. Now let us just lift up **our hearts with gratitude** for a few moments. Here we are to-night; we know that we are guilty, but our sins have all been punished years ago. Before my soul believed in Christ, the punishment of my sin had all been endured. We are not to think that Christ's blood derives its

6

efficacy from our faith. *Fact precedes faith.* Though still defiled by sin, yet who can lay anything to the charge of the man whose guilt is gone, lifted bodily from off him, and put upon Christ? How can any punishment fall on that man who ceases to possess sins, because his sin has eighteen hundred years ago been cast upon Christ, and Christ has suffered in his place and stead? Oh, glorious triumph of faith to be able to say, whenever I feel the guilt of sin, whenever conscience pricks me, "Yes, it is true, but my Lord is answerable for it all, for He has taken it all upon Himself, and suffered in my place."

III. You see then the reality of the imputation of sin to Christ from the amazing doctrine that Christ is made sin for us. But now notice the concluding thought, upon which I must dwell a moment, but it must be very briefly, for two reasons, my time has gone, and my strength has gone too.

"That we might be made the righteousness of God in Him."

Now, here I beg you to notice, that it does not simply say that we might be made *righteous*, but "that we might be made **the righteousness** of God in Him;" as if righteousness, that lovely, glorious,

God-honouring, God-delighting thing—as if we were
actually made *that*. God looks on His people as being
abstract righteousness, not only righteous, but
righteousness. To be righteous, is as if a man should
have a box covered with gold, the box would then be
golden; but to be righteous*ness* is to have a box of
solid gold. To be a righteous man is to have righteousness cast over me; but to be made righteousness, that
is to be made solid essential righteousness in the sight
of God. Well now, this is a glorious fact and a most
wonderful privilege, that we poor sinners are made
"the righteousness of God in Him. " God sees no sin
in any one of His people, no iniquity in Jacob, when
He looks upon them in Christ. In themselves He sees
nothing but filth and abomination, in Christ nothing
but purity and righteousness.

Is it not, and must it not ever be to the Christian,
one of his most delightful privileges to know that
altogether apart from anything that we have ever
done, or can do, God looks upon His people as being
righteous, nay, as being righteousness, and that
despite all the sins they have ever committed, they
are accepted in Him as if they had been Christ, while
Christ was punished for them as if He had been sin.

Oh, Christian, get thee up, get thee up into the high

mountain, and stand where thy Saviour stands, for that is thy place. Lie not there on the dunghill of fallen humanity, that is not thy place now; Christ has once taken it on thy behalf. "He made Him to be sin for us." Thy place is yonder there, above the starry hosts, where He hath raised us up together, and made us sit together in Heavenly places in Him. Not there, at the day of judgment, where the wicked shreik for shelter, and beg for the hills to cover them, but there, where Jesus sits upon His throne—there is thy place, my soul. He will make thee to sit upon His throne, even as He has overcome, and has sat down with His Father upon His throne.

He wore my crown, the crown of thorns; I wear his crown, the crown of glory. He wore my dress, nay, rather, he wore my nakedness when He died upon the Cross; I wear His robes, the royal robes of the King of kings. He bore my shame; I bear His honour. He endured my sufferings to this end that my joy be full, and that His joy may be fulfilled in me. He lay in the grave that I might rise from the dead and that I may dwell in Him, and all this He comes again to give me, to make it sure to me and to all that love His appearing, to shew that all His people shall enter into their inheritance.

None but Jesus

"He that believeth on Him is not condemned" (John 3. 18).

THE way of salvation is stated in Scripture in the very plainest terms, and yet, perhaps, there is no truth about which more errors have been uttered, than concerning the faith which saves the soul. So plain is Scripture, that one would have said, "He that runs may read;" but so dim is man's eye, and so marred is his understanding, that the very simplest truth of Scripture he distorts and misrepresents.

I intend, by God's help, to put together sundry thoughts upon faith, each of which have been misunderstood from the want of their having been put together in their proper consecutive order. I shall speak a little on each of these points; first, *the object of faith*, to what it looks; next, *the reason of faith*, whence it comes; thirdly, *the ground of faith*, or what it wears when it comes; fourthly, *the warrant of faith*, or why it dares to come to Christ; and fifthly, *the result of faith*, or, how it speeds when it doth come to Christ.

I. First, then,

The Object of Faith,

or to what faith looks.

I am told in the Word of God to believe—What am
I to believe? I am bidden to look—at what am I to
look? What is to be the object of my hope, belief,
and confidence? The reply is simple. The object of
Faith to a sinner is Christ Jesus. How many make a
mistake about this and think that they are to believe
on *God the Father*! Now belief in God is an after-
result of faith in Jesus. We come to believe in the
eternal love of the Father as the result of trusting the
precious Blood of the Son. I know your salvation
depends on the whole Trinity, yet the first and im-
mediate object of a sinner's justifying faith is neither
God the Father nor God the Holy Ghost, but *God the
Son*, incarnate in human flesh, and offering atonement
for sinners. Hast thou the eye of faith? Then, soul,
look thou to *Christ as God*. If thou wouldst be saved,
believe Him to be *God* over all, blessed for ever. Bow
before Him, and accept Him as being "Very God of
very God," for if thou do not, thou hast no part in
Him. When thou hast thus believed, believe in Him
as *Man*. Believe the wondrous story of His incarnation; rely upon the testimony of the evangelists, who

declare that the Infinite was robed in the infant, that
the Eternal was concealed within the mortal; that He
who was King of Heaven became a Servant of servants
and the Son of man. Believe and admire the mystery
of His incarnation, for unless thou believe this, thou
canst not be saved thereby.

But take care that thy faith mainly fixes itself upon
Christ *as dying and as dead*. View the Lamb of God as
dumb before His shearers; view Him as the Man of
Sorrows and acquainted with grief; go thou with Him
to Gethsemane, and behold Him sweating drops of
blood. Mark, thy faith has nothing to do with anything within thyself; the object of thy faith is nothing
within thee, but a something without thee. Believe
on Him, then, who on yonder Tree with nailed hands
and feet pours out His life for sinners. There is the
object of thy faith for justification; not in thyself, nor
in anything which the Holy Spirit has done in thee, nor
anything He has promised to do for thee; but thou art
to look to Christ and to Christ Jesus alone.

Then let thy faith behold Christ as *rising from the
dead*. See Him—He has borne the curse, and now He
receives the justification. He dies to pay the debt;
He rises that He may nail the handwriting of that
discharged debt to the Cross. See Him ascending up

on high, and behold Him this day pleading before the Father's throne. He is there pleading for His people, offering up to-day His authoritative petition for all that come to God by Him. And He, as God, as Man, as living, as dying, as rising, and as reigning above— He, and He alone, is to be the object of thy faith for the pardon of sin.

Christ has endured once for all, and put away their sins for ever by the sacrifice of Himself. Now this is the great object of faith. I pray you, do not make any mistake about this, for a mistake here will be dangerous, if not fatal. View Christ, by your faith, as being in His life, and death, and sufferings, and resurrection, the substitute for all whom His Father gave Him—the vicarious sacrifice for the sins of all those who will trust Him with their souls. Christ, then, thus set forth, is the object of justifying faith.

Now let me further remark that there are some of you, no doubt, saying: "Oh, I should believe and I should be saved if—" If what? If Christ had died? "Oh, no, sir, my doubt is nothing about Christ." I thought so. Then what is the doubt? "Why, I should believe *if I felt this, or if I had done that.*" Just so; but I tell you, you can not believe in Jesus if you felt that, or if you had done that, for then you

would believe in yourself, and not in Christ. That is
the English of it. If you were so-and-so, or so-and-so,
then you could have confidence. Confidence in what?
Why, confidence in your feelings, and confidence in
your doings, and that is just the clear contrary of
confidence in Christ? Faith is not to infer from something good within me that I shall be saved, but to
say in the teeth, and despite of the fact that I am guilty
in the sight of God and deserve His wrath, yet I do
nevertheless believe that the Blood of Jesus Christ
His Son cleanseth me from all sin; and though my
present consciousness condemns me, yet my faith
overpowers my consciousness, and I do believe that
"He is able to save to the uttermost them that come
unto God by Him." To come to Christ as a saint is a
very easy work; to trust to a doctor to cure you when
you believe you are getting better, is very easy; but
to trust your physician when you feel as if the sentence
of death were in your body, to bear up when the
disease is rising into the very skin, and when the ulcer
is gathering its venom—to believe even then in the
efficacy of the medicine—that is faith. And so, when
sin gets the mastery of thee, when thou feelest that the
law condemns thee, then, even then, as a sinner, to
trust Christ, this is the most daring feat in all the

world; and the faith which shook down the walls of Jericho, the faith which raised the dead, the faith which stopped the mouths of lions, was not greater than that of a poor sinner, when in the teeth of all his sins he dares to trust the Blood and righteousness of Jesus Christ. Do this, soul, then thou art saved whosoever thou mayest be. The object of faith, then, is Christ as the substitute for sinners. God in Christ, but not God apart from Christ, nor any work of the Spirit, but the work of Jesus only must be viewed by you as the foundation of your hope.

II. And now, secondly,

The Reason of Faith,

or why doth any man believe, and whence doeth his faith come?

"Faith cometh by *hearing*" (Rom. 10. 17). Granted, but do not all men hear, and do not many still remain unbelieving? How, then, doth any man come by his faith? To his own experience his faith comes as the result of *a sense of need*. He feels himself needing a Saviour; he finds Christ to be just such a Saviour as he wants, and therefore because he cannot help himself, he believes in Jesus. Having nothing of his own, he feels he must take Christ or else perish, and therefore he doth it because he cannot help doing it. He is fairly driven up into a corner, and there is but this one way of escape, namely, by the righteousness of another; for he feels he cannot escape by any good deeds, or sufferings of his own, and he cometh to Christ and humbleth himself, because he cannot do without Christ, and must perish unless he lay hold of Him.

But to carry the question further back, where does that man get his sense of need? How is it that *he*, rather than others, feels his need of Christ? It is certain he has no more necessity for Christ than other men. How doth he come to know, then, that he is lost and ruined? How is it that he is driven by the sense of ruin to take hold on Christ the restorer? The reply is, this is *the gift of God*; this is the work of the Spirit. No man comes to Christ except the Spirit draw him, and the Spirit draws men to Christ by shutting them up under the law to a conviction that if they do not come to Christ they must perish. Then by sheer stress of weather, they tack about and run into this Heavenly port. Salvation by Christ is so disagreeable to our carnal mind, so inconsistent with our love of human merit, that we never would take Christ to be our all in all, if the Spirit did not convince us that we were nothing at all, and did not so compel us to lay hold on Christ.

III. But now I shall want your careful attention, while I come to another point, upon which you, perhaps, will think I contradict myself, and that is,

The Ground of the Sinner's Faith,

or on what ground he dares to believe on the Lord Jesus Christ.

I have already said that no man will believe in Jesus unless he feels his need of Him. But I do not come to Christ pleading that I feel my need of Him; my reason for believing in Christ is not that I *feel* my need of Him, but that I *have* a need of Him. The ground on which a man comes to Jesus is not as a sensible sinner, but as a sinner, and nothing but a sinner. He will not come unless he is awakened; but when he comes, he does not say, "Lord, I come to Thee because I am an awakened sinner; save me. " But he says, "Lord, I am a sinner; save me. " Not his awakening, but his sinnership is the method and plan upon which he dares to come. When I come to Jesus, I know I am not come unless I am awakened, but still, I do not come *as* an awakened sinner. I do not stand at the foot of the Cross to be washed because I

have repented; I bring nothing when I come but sin.
A sense of need is a good feeling, but when I stand at
the foot of the Cross, I do not believe in Christ because
I have got good feelings, but I believe in Him whether
I have good feelings or not.

> "Just as I am, without one plea,
> But that Thy Blood was shed for me,
> And that Thou bidst me come to thee,
> O Lamb of God, I come."

The gate of Mercy is opened, and over the door it is
written, "This is a faithful saying and worthy of all
acceptation, that Christ Jesus came into the world to
save *sinners*" (1 Tim. 1. 15).   Between that word
"save" and the next word "sinners," there is no
adjective.   It does not say, "penitent sinners,"
"awakened sinners," "sensible sinners," "grieving
sinners," or "alarmed sinners."   No, it only says,
"sinners," and I know this, that when I come, I come
to Christ to-day, for I feel it is as much a necessity of
my life to come to the Cross of Christ to-day as it
was to come ten years ago—when I come to Him I
dare not come as a conscious sinner or an awakened
sinner, but I have to come still as a sinner with
nothing in my hands.

The ground on which a sinner comes to Christ is
that he is black; that he is dead, and not that he

knows he is dead; that he is lost, and not that he knows
he is lost.   I know he will not come unless he does
know it, but that is not the ground on which he comes.
It is the secret reason why, but it is not the public
positive ground which he understands.   Here was I,
year after year, afraid to come to Christ because I
thought I did not feel enough; and I used to read that
hymn of Cowper's about being insensible as steel:

> "If aught is felt, 'tis only pain
> To find I cannot feel."

When I believed in Christ, I thought I did not feel
at all.   *Now* when I look back I find that I had been
feeling all the while most acutely and intensely, and
most of all because I thought I did not feel.   Generally
the people who repent the most, think they are impenitent, and people feel most their need when they
think they do not feel at all, for we are no judges of
our feelings, and hence the Gospel invitation is not
put upon the ground of anything of which we can be a
judge; it is put on the ground of our being sinners and
nothing but sinners.

"Well," says one, "but it says, 'Come unto Me
all ye that are weary and heavy-laden, and I will give
you rest'—then we must be weary and heavy-laden."
Just so; so it is in that text, but then there is another.

"Whosoever will let him come;" and that does not
say anything about "weary and heavy-laden." Besides, while the invitation is given to the weary and
heavy-laden, you will perceive that the promise is not
made to them *as* weary and heavy-laden, but it is
made to them *as* coming to Christ. They did not know
that they were weary and heavy-laden when they came
they thought they were not. They really were, but
part of their weariness was that they could not be as
weary as they would like to be, and part of their load
was that they did not feel their load enough. They
came to Christ just as they were, and He saved them,
not because there was any merit in their weariness, or
any efficacy in their being heavy-laden, but He saved
them as sinners and nothing but sinners, and so they
were washed in His Blood and made clean.

IV. But not to stay longer, my fourth point has
to do with

The Warrant of Faith,

or why a man dares to trust in Christ.

Is it not imprudent for any man to trust Christ to
save him, and especially when he has no good thing
whatever? Is it not an arrogant presumption for any
man to trust Christ? No, sirs, it is not. It is a grand
and noble work of God the Holy Spirit for a man to

give the lie to all his sins, and still to believe and set
to his seal that God is true, and believe in the virtue
of the Blood of Jesus. But why does any man dare to
believe in Christ I will ask you now. "Well," saith
one man, "I summoned faith to believe in Christ
because I did feel there was a work of the Spirit in me."
You do not believe in Christ at all. "Well," says
another, "I thought that I had a *right* to believe in
Christ, because I felt somewhat." You had not any
right to believe in Christ at all on such a warranty as
that. What is a man's warrant then for believing in
Christ. Here it is. Christ tells him to do it that is
his warrant. Christ's word is the warrant of the
sinner for believing in Christ—not what he *feels* nor
what he *is*, nor what he *is not*, but that Christ has told
him to do it. The Gospel runs thus: "Believe on the
Lord Jesus Christ and thou shalt be saved. He that
believeth not shall be damned."

Faith in Christ then is a commanded duty as well as
a blessed privilege, and what a mercy it is that it is a
duty; because there never can be any question but
that a man has a right to do his duty. Now on the
ground that God commands me to believe, I have a
right to believe, be I who I may.

The Gospel is sent to every creature. Well, I

belong to that tribe; I am one of the every creatures,
and that Gospel commands me to believe and I do it.
I cannot have done wrong in doing it, for I was commanded to do so. I cannot be wrong in obeying a
command of God. Now it is a command of God given
to every creature that he should believe on Jesus
Christ whom God hath sent. This is your warrant,
sinner, and a blessed warrant it is, for it is one which
Hell cannot gainsay, and which Heaven cannot
withdraw. You need not be looking within to look
for the misty warrants of your experience, you need
not be looking to your works, and to your feelings,
to get some dull and insufficient warrants for your
confidence in Christ. You may believe Christ because
He tells you to do so. That is a sure ground to stand
on, and one which admits of no doubts.

Sinner, you cannot be lost by trusting Christ, but
you will be lost if you do not trust Him, ay, and lost
for not trusting Him. I put it boldly now—sinner,
not only may you come, but oh! I pray you, do not
defy the wrath of God by refusing to come. The gate
of mercy stands wide open; why will you not come?
Why will you not? Why so proud? Why will you
still refuse His voice and perish in your sins? Mark,
if you perish, any one of you, your blood lies not at
  7

God's door, nor Christ's door, but at your own. He can say of you, "Ye will not come unto Me that ye might have life." Oh! poor trembler, if thou be willing to come, there is nothing in God's Word to keep thee from coming, but there are both threatenings to drive thee, and power to draw thee.

Still I hear you say, "I must not trust Christ." You *may*, I say, for every creature under Heaven is commanded to do it, and what you are commanded to do, you may do. "Ah! well," saith one, "still I do not feel that I may." There you are again; you say you will not do what God tells you, because of some stupid feelings of your own. You are not told to trust Christ because you feel anything, but simply because you are a sinner. Now you know you are a sinner. "I am," says one, "and that is my sorrow." Why your sorrow? That is some sign that you do feel. "Ay," saith one, "but I do not feel enough, and that is why I sorrow. I do not feel as I should." Well, suppose you do feel, or suppose you do not, you are a sinner, and "this is a faithful saying and worthy of all acceptation that Christ Jesus came into the world to save sinners." "Oh, but I am such an old sinner; I have been sixty years in sin." Where is it written that after sixty you cannot be saved? Sir, Christ

could save you at a hundred—ay, if you were a
Methuselah in guilt. "The Blood of Jesus Christ His
Son cleanseth us from all sin." "Whosoever will let
him come." "He is able to save to the uttermost
them that come unto God by Him" (Heb. 7. 25).
"Yes," says one, "but I have been a drunkard, a
swearer, or lascivious, or profane." Then you are a
sinner, you have not gone further than the uttermost,
and He is able to save you still. "Ay," saith another,
"but you do not know how my guilt has been ag-
gravated." That only proves you to be a sinner, and
that you are commanded to trust Christ and be saved.
"Ay," cries yet another, "but you do not know how
often I have rejected Christ." Yes, but that only
makes you the more a sinner. "You do not know how
hard my heart is." Just so, but that only proves you
to be a sinner, and still proves you to be one whom
Christ came to save. "Oh, but, sir, I have not any
good thing. If I had, you know, I should have something to encourage me." The fact of your not having
any good thing just proves to me that you are the man
I am sent to preach to. Christ came to save that which
was lost, and all you have said only proves that you
are lost, and therefore He came to save you. Do trust
Him; do trust Him. "But if I am saved," saith one,

"I shall be the biggest sinner that ever was saved." Then the greater music in Heaven when you get there; the more glory to Christ, for the bigger the sinner the more honour to Christ when at last he shall be brought home. "Ay, but my sin has abounded." His grace shall much more abound. "But my sin has reached even to Heaven." Yes, but His mercy reaches above the Heavens. "Oh! but my guilt is as broad as the world." Yes, but His righteousness is broader than a thousand worlds. "Ay, but my sin is scarlet." Yes, but His Blood is more scarlet than your sins, and can wash the scarlet out by a richer scarlet. "Ay! but I deserve to be lost, and death and Hell cry for my damnation." Yes, and so they may, but the Blood of Jesus Christ can cry louder than either death or Hell; and it cries to-day, "Father, let the sinner live." Oh! I wish I could get this thought out of my mouth, and get it into your heads, that when God saves you, it is not because of anything in you, it is because of something in Himself. God's love has no reason except in His own bowels; God's reason for pardoning a sinner is found in His own heart, and not in the sinner. And there is as much reason in you why you should be saved as why another should be saved, namely, no reason at all. There is no reason in you why He should have mercy on you, but there is no reason wanted, for the reason lies in God and in God alone.

V. And now I come to the conclusion, and I trust you will have patience with me, for my last point is a very glorious one, and full of joy to those souls who as sinners dare to believe in Christ—

The Result of Faith,

or how it speeds when it comes to Christ.

The text says, "He that believeth is not condemned." There is a man there who has just this moment believed; he is not condemned. But he has been fifty years in sin, and has plunged into all manner of vice; his sins, which are many, are all forgiven him. He stands in the sight of God now as innocent as though he had never sinned. Such is the power of Jesus' Blood, that "he that believeth is not condemned." Does this relate to what is to happen at the day of Judgment? I pray you look at the text, and you will find it does not say, "He that believeth *shall* not be condemned," but he *is* not; he is not *now*. And if he is not now, then it follows that he never shall be; for having believed in Christ that promise still stands, "He that believeth is not condemned."

I believe to-day I am not condemned; in fifty years'
time that promise will be just the same—"He that
believeth is not condemned." So that the moment a
man puts his trust in Christ, he is freed from all condemnation—past, present, and to come; and from
that day he stands in God's sight as though he were
without spot or wrinkle, or any such thing.

"But he sins," you say. He does indeed, but his
sins are not laid to his charge. They were laid to the
charge of Christ of old, and God can never charge the
offence on two—first on Christ, and then on the sinner.
"Ay, but he often falls into sin." That may be
possible; though if the Spirit of God be in him he
sinneth not as he was wont to do. He sins by reason
of infirmity, not by reason of his love to sin, for now
he hateth it. But mark, you shall put it in your own
way if you will, and I will answer, "Yes, but though
he sin, yet is he no more guilty in the sight of God, for
all his guilt has been taken from him, and put on
Christ—positively, literally, and actually lifted off
from him, and put upon Jesus Christ."

Do you see the Jewish host? There is a scapegoat
brought out; the high priest confesses the sin of the
people over the scapegoat's head. The sin is all gone
from the people, and laid upon the scapegoat. Away

goes the scapegoat into the wilderness. Is there
any sin felt on the people? If there be, then the scapegoat has not carried it away. Because it cannot be
here and *there* too. It cannot be carried away and left
behind too. "No," say you, "Scripture says the
scapegoat carried away the sin; there was none left
on the people when the scapegoat had taken away the
sin. And so, when by faith we put our hand upon the
head of Christ, does Christ take away our sin, or does
He not? If He does not, then it is of no use our believing in Him; but if He doth really take away our sin,
then our sin cannot be on Him and on us too, if it be on
Christ, we are free, clear, accepted, justified, and this
is the true doctrine of justification by faith. As soon
as a man believeth in Christ Jesus, his sins are gone
from him, and gone away for ever. They are blotted
out now.

What if a man had owed a hundred pounds, if he has
got a receipt for it, he is free; it is blotted out; there
is an erasure made in the book, and the debt is gone.
Though the man commit sin, yet the debt having been
paid before even the debt was acquired, he is no more
a debtor to the law of God. Doth not Scripture say,
that God has cast His people's sins into the depths
of the sea. Now, if they are in the depths of the sea,

they cannot be on His people too. Blessed be His Name, in the day when He casts our sins into the depth of the sea, He views us as pure in His sight, and we stand accepted in the Beloved. Then He says, "As far as the east is from the west, so far hath He removed our transgressions from us" (Psa. 103. 12). They cannot be removed and be here still. Then if thou believest in Christ, thou art no more in the sight of God a sinner; thou art accepted as though thou wert perfect, as though thou hadst kept the law—for Christ has kept it, and His righteousness is thine. You have broken it, but your sin is His, and He has been punished for it. Mistake not yourselves any longer; you are no more what you were; when you believe, you stand in Christ's stead, even as Christ of old stood in your stead. The transformation is complete, the exchange is positive and eternal. They who believe in Jesus are as much accepted of God the Father as even His Eternal Son is accepted; and they that believe not, let them do what they will, they shall but go about to work out their own righteousness; but they abide under the law, and still shall they be under the curse.

Now, ye that believe in Jesus, walk up and down the earth in the glory of this great truth. You are sinners in yourselves, but you are washed in the Blood of Christ. David says, "Wash me, and I shall be whiter than snow" (Psa. 51. 7). You have lately seen the snow come down—how clear! how white! What could be whiter? Why, the Christian is whiter than that. You say, "He is black." I know he is as black as anyone—as black as Hell—but the blood-drop falls on him, and he is as white—"whiter than snow." The next time you see the snow-white crystals falling from Heaven, look on them and say, "Ah! though I must confess within myself that I am un-worthy and unclean, yet, believing in Christ, He hath given me His righteousness so completely, that I am even whiter than the snow as it descends from the treasury of God." Oh! for faith to lay hold on this. Oh! for an overpowering faith that shall get the victory over doubts and fears, and make us enjoy the liberty wherewith Christ makes men free.

Fully absolved, by grace you shall be found at last and all sin's tremendous curse and blame shall be taken away, not because of anything you have done. I pray you do all you can for Christ out of gratitude, but even when you have done all, do not rest there. Rest still in the substitution and the sacrifice. Be you what Christ was in His Father's sight, and when

conscience awakens, you can tell it that Christ was
for you all that you ought to have been, that He has
suffered all your penalty; and now neither mercy nor
justice can smite you, since justice has clasped hands
with mercy in a firm decree to save that man whose
faith is in the Cross of Christ.   The Lord bless these
words for His sake.   AMEN.

God's Five Negatives

"He hath said, I will never leave thee, nor forsake thee"
(Heb. 13. 5).

WE turn with great pleasure, to the wonderful words of our text, "He hath said, I will *never* leave thee, nor forsake thee." I have no doubt you are aware that our translation does not convey the whole force of the original, and that it would hardly be possible in English to give the full weight of the Greek. We might render it, "He hath said, I will *never, never* leave thee; I will *never, never, never* forsake thee;" for, though that would be not a literal, but rather a free rendering, yet, as there are five negatives in the Greek, we do not know how to give their force in any other way. Two negatives nullify each other in our language; but here, in the Greek, they intensify the meaning following one after another, as I suppose David's five stones out of the brook would have done if the first had not been enough to make the giant reel. The verse we sung just now is a very good rendering of the original:

"The soul that on Jesus hath lean'd for repose,
  I will not, I will not desert to his foes;
  That soul, though all hell should endeavour to shake,
  I'll *never*, no *never*, no *never* forsake."

Here you have the five negatives very well placed, and the force of the Greek, as nearly as possible, given.

In trying to expound this fivefold assurance, this quintessence of consolation, we shall have to draw your attention:

I. First of all to

An Awful Condition

—lost and forsaken of God! I am quite certain I shall fail in attempting to describe this state of mind. I have thought of it, dreamed of it, and felt it in such feeble measure as a child of God can feel it, but how to describe it I know not.

1. Forsaking implies **an utter loneliness.** Put a traveller in a vast howling wilderness, where for many a league there is no trace of man—no footstep of traveller. The solitary wretch cries for help—the hollow echo of the rocks is his only reply. No bird in the air; not even a prowling jackal in the waste; not an insect in the sunbeam to keep him company; not even a solitary blade of grass to remind him of God! Yet, even there he is not alone: for yon bare rocks prove a God, and the hot sand beneath his feet, and

the blazing sun above his head, all witness to a present Deity.

But what would be the loneliness of a man forsaken of God! No migration could be so awful as this, for he says, "If I *take* the wings of the morning and dwell in the uttermost parts of the sea" *Thou art there* (Psa. 139. 9). Such a state were worse than Hell, for David says, "If I make my bed in Hell, *Thou art there*" (Psa. 139. 8). Loneliness is a feeling which none of us delight in. Solitude may have some charms, but they who are forced to be her captives have not discovered them. A transient solitude may give pleasure; to be alone, utterly alone, is terrible; to be alone, *without God*, is such an emphasis of loneliness, that I defy the lip even of a lost spirit to express the horror and anguish that must be concentrated in it.

There is far more than you and I dream of in the language of our Lord Jesus, when He says: "My God, why hast Thou forsaken Me?" is the cry of uttermost dismay. Thank God, you and I by this promise are taught that we never shall know the desperate loneliness of being forsaken of God; yet, this is what it would be if He should forsake us!

2. Mingling with this mournful solitude is a sense of **utter helplessness**. Power belongeth unto God;

withdraw the Lord, and the strong men must utterly fail. The archangel without God passes away and is not; the everlasting hills do bow, and the solid pillars of the earth are dissolved. Without God our dust returneth to the earth; without God our spirit mourneth like David, "I am forgotten as a dead man out of mind; I am like a broken vessel" (Psa. 31. 12).

Christ knew what this was when He said, "I am a worm, and no man" (Psa. 22. 6). He was so utterly broken, so emptied of all power, that as He hung with dislocated limbs upon the Cross, He cried, "My strength is dried up like a potsherd; thou hast brought Me into the dust of death." No broken reed or smoking flax can be so feeble as a soul forsaken of God.

Glorious are those negatives which shut us in from all fear of this calamity.

3. To be forsaken of God implies **utter friendlessness**. A thousand times let Jehovah be blessed that very few of us have ever known what it is to be friendless! There have been times in the experience of some when we felt that we stood without a friend in the particular spot which we then occupied, for we had a grief which we could not entrust to any other heart.

As long as a man feels he has some one loving him, he has something worth living for; but when the last friend is gone and we feel that we are floating on a raft far out at sea, with not a sail in sight, and we cry, "Welcome death!" Our Lord and Master was brought to this state, and knew what it was to be forsaken, for He had no friends left. "He that eateth bread with Me hath lifted up his heel against Me."

Oh, may you and I never know it! To be without a friend in Heaven; to look to that throne of glory and to see the blackness of darkness there; to turn to mercy and receive a frown; to fly to love and receive a rebuke; to turn to God and find that His ear is heavy that He will not hear, and His hand restrained that He will not help—oh! this is terror, terror heaped on terror, to be thus *forsaken*!

4. Loneliness, helplessness, friendlessness—add these together, and then put the next—**hopelessness**. A man forsaken of men may still entertain some hope. But let him be forsaken of God, and then hope hath failed; the last window is shut; not a ray of light now streams into the thick Egyptian darkness of his mind. Life is death; death is damnation—damnation in its lowest deeps. Let him look to men, and they are broken reeds; let him turn to angels, and

they are avengers; let him look to death, and even the
tomb affords no refuge. Look where he will, blank,
black despair seizes hold upon him.

5. To make up this fivefold forsaking, against
which we have the five negatives, let us add to all this
loneliness, helplessness, friendlessness, and hopelessness, a sense of **unutterable agony**. We speak of
agony, but to feel it is a very different thing. Misery
and despair—the *wrestling* of these with the spirit till
the spirit is trodden down, and crushed, and broken,
and chooses strangling rather than life; a horrible
sense of every evil having made one's heart its den; a
consciousness that we are the target for all God's
arrows; that *all* God's waves and billows have gone
over us; that He hath forgotten to be gracious; that
He will be merciful to us no more; that He hath in
anger shut up the bowels of His compassion—this is a
part of being forsaken of God which only lost spirits
can know.

When we thus describe being forsaken of God, is it
not satisfactory to the highest degree to remember
that we have God's Word for it five times over, "I
will *never*, *never* leave thee; I will *never*, *never*, *never*
forsake thee?"

II. We have before us now, in the second place,

a gracious promise, or what is positively guaranteed.

What is guaranteed in this promise? Beloved, herein doth God give to His people everything. "*I will never leave thee.*" Then no attribute of God can cease to be engaged for us. Is He mighty? He will show Himself strong on the behalf of them that trust Him. Is He love? Then with everlasting loving-kindness will He have mercy upon us. Whatever attributes may compose the character of Deity every one of them to its fullest extent shall be engaged on our side. Moreover, whatsoever God hath, whether it be in the lowest Hades or in the highest Heaven, whatever can be contained in infinity or can be held within the circumference of eternity, whatever, in fine, can be in Him who filleth all things, and yet is greater than all things, shall be with His people for ever, since "He hath said, *I* will *never* leave you, nor forsake you." How one might enlarge here, but I forbear; ye yourselves know that to sum up "all things" is a task beyond all human might.

III. More fully, however, to expound this promise, I would remind you of the five occasions in which it occurs in Scripture. The number five runs all through our subject. The sense and spirit of the text are to be found in innumerable places, and

8

possibly there may be some other passages which
approximate so very nearly to our text, that you
might say they also are repetitions, but I think there
are five which may clearly take the priority

The Case of Jacob.

1. One of the first instances is to be found in
Genesis 28. 15.   "Behold, I am with thee, and will
keep thee in all places whither thou goest, and will
bring thee again into this land; for I will not leave
thee, until I have done that which I have spoken to
thee of."   Here we have this promise in the case of
a man of trials.   More than either Abraham or Isaac,
JACOB was the son of tribulation.   He was now flying
away from his father's house, leaving the over-
fondness of a mother's attachment, abhorred by his
elder brother, who sought his blood.   He lies down to
sleep, with a stone for his pillow, with the hedges for
his curtains, with the earth for his bed, and the
heavens for his canopy; and as he sleeps thus friendless,
solitary, and alone, God saith to him, "I will *never,
never* leave thee."

Mark his after career.   He is guided to Padan-
aram; God, his Guide, leaves him not.   At Padan-
aram Laban cheats him, wickedly and wrongfully

cheats him in many ways; but God doth not leave
him, and he is more than a match for the thievish
Laban. He flies at last with his wives and children;
Laban, in hot haste pursues him, but the Lord does
not leave him; Mizpah's Mount bears witness that
God can stop the pursuer, and change the foe into a
friend. Esau comes against him; let Jabbok testify
to Jacob's wrestlings, and through the power of him
who never did forsake His servant, Esau kisses his
brother, whom once he thought to slay. Anon Jacob
dwells in tents and booths at Succoth; he journeys
up and down throughout the land, and his sons
treacherously slay the Shechemites. Then the nations round about seek to avenge their death, but the
Lord again interposes, and Jacob is delivered.

Poor Jacob is bereaved of his sons. He cries:
"Joseph is not, and Simeon is not, and now ye will
take Benjamin away; all these things are against me"
(Gen. 42. 36). But they are not against him; God
has not left him, for He has not yet done everything
that He had spoken to him of. The old man goes into
Egypt; his lips are refreshed while he kisses the cheeks
of his favourite Joseph, and until the last, when he
gathers up his feet in the bed and sings of that coming
Shiloh and the sceptre that should not depart from

Judah, good old Jacob proves that in six troubles
God is with His people, and in seven He doth not
forsake them; that even to hoar hairs He is the same,
and until old age He doth carry them.

You Jacobs, full of affliction, you tried and troubled
heirs of Heaven, He hath said to you, each one of you
—oh! believe Him!—"I will *never* leave thee; I will
never forsake thee."

The Case of Moses.

2. The next instance in which we find this same
promise is in Deuteronomy 31. 6. Here we find it
spoken, not so much to individuals as to the whole
body collectively.¹ MOSES said unto the people of
Judah, by the Word of God, "Be strong, and of a
good courage, fear not, nor be afraid of them: for the
Lord thy God, He it is that doth go with thee; He will
not fail thee, nor *forsake* thee." These people were to
fight the accursed nations of Canaan, to drive out the
giants, and the men who had chariots of iron, but the
Lord said He would never leave them, nor did He, till
from Dan to Beersheba the favoured race possessed
the promised land, and the tribes went up to Jerusalem
with the voice of joyful song.

I would it were my lot yet more and more, like

Joshua, to lead you from one place to another, smiting the enemies of the Lord and extending the kingdom of Messias! Let us undertake what we may, we shall never fail. Let us by faith, love great things, and we shall do great things. Let us venture upon notable exploits which shall seem fanatical to reason and absurd to men of prudence, for He hath said, "I will *never* leave you nor *forsake* you. "

The Case of Joshua.

3. The third occasion upon which this promise was made is in Joshua 1. 5, where the Lord says to JOSHUA, "There shall not any man be able to stand before thee all the days of thy life; as I was with Moses, so I will be with thee: I will *not fail* thee, nor *forsake* thee. " It needs not that I should tell you that it is not every man who can stand first in the ranks, and that, albeit there is no small share of honour given by God to such a man, yet there is a bitterness in His lot which no other men can know. There are times when, if it were not for faith, we would give up the ghost, and, were not the Master with us, we would turn our back and fly, like Jonah, unto Nineveh. But if any of you be called to occupy prominent positions in God's Church, bind this about your arm and it shall make

you strong; He hath said to you, "I will *never* leave
thee, nor *forsake* thee. " "Go, in this thy might;
the Lord is with thee, thou mighty man of valour"
(Judges 6. 14).

The Case of Solomon.

4. On the next occasion, this same promise was
given by David in his last moments to his son SOLOMON
(1 Chronicles 28. 20). David was speaking of what he
himself by experience had proved to be true, and he
declares: "Be strong and of good courage, and do it:
fear not, nor be dismayed: for the Lord God, even my
God, will be with thee; he will *not fail* thee, nor
forsake thee, until thou hast finished all the work for
the service of the house of the Lord. "

Some Christians are placed where they need much
prudence, discretion, and wisdom. You may take this
for your promise. The Queen of Sheba came to see
Solomon; she put to him many difficult questions,
but God did not leave him, nor forsake him, and he
was able to answer them all. As judge over Israel,
many knotty points were brought before him; you
remember the child and the mothers, and how wisely
he decided the case. The building of the temple was
a very mighty work—the like of which the earth had

never seen, but, by wisdom given to him, the stones were fashioned, and laid one upon another, till at last the top stone was brought out with shoutings.

You shall do the same, O man of business, though yours be a very responsible situation. You shall finish your course, O careful worker, though there are many eyes that watch for your halting. You shall do the same, sister, though you need to have seven eyes rather than two; you shall hear the voice of God saying: "This is the way, walk ye in it." Thou shalt never be ashamed nor confounded, world without end.

The Case of the Unknown.

5. Once more, and perhaps this fifth occasion may be the most comforting to the most of you, Isaiah 41. 17: "When the poor and needy seek water, and there is none, and their tongue faileth for thirst, I the Lord will hear them, I the God of Israel will *not forsake* them." You may be brought to this state to-day. Your soul may *need Christ*, but you may not be able to find Him. You may feel that without the mercy which comes from the atoning Blood you are lost. You may have gone to works and ceremonies, to prayings and doings, to alms-givings and to experiences, and have found them all dried wells, and

now you can hardly pray, for your tongue cleaves to
the roof of your mouth for thirst. Now in your worst
condition, brought to the lowest state into which a
creature ever can be cast, *Christ will not forsake you,
He will appear for your help*.

Surely one of these five occasions must suit you,
and let me here remind you that whatever God has said
to any one Saint He has said to all. When He opens
a well for one man it is that all may drink. When the
Manna falls, it is not only for those in the wilderness,
but we by faith do eat the Manna still. No promise
is of private interpretation. When God openeth a
granary-door to give out food, there may be some one
starving man who is the occasion of its being opened,
but all the hungry besides may come and feed too.

Whether He gave the word to Abraham or to Moses
matters not; He has given it to thee as one of the
covenanted seed. There is not a high blessing too
lofty for thee; nor a wide mercy too extensive for thee.
Lift up now thine eyes to the north and to the south,
to the east and to the west, for all this is thine. Climb
to Pisgah's top, and view the utmost limit of the
Divine promise, for the land is all thine own. There
is not a brook of living water of which thou mayest
not drink. If the land floweth with milk and honey,

eat the honey and drink the milk. The fattest of the kine, yea, and the sweetest of the wines, let all be thine, for there is no denial of any one of them to any saint. Be thou bold to believe, for He hath said, "I will *never* leave *thee*, nor forsake *thee.*"

To put everything in one, there is nothing you can want, there is nothing you can ask for, there is nothing you can need in time or in eternity, there is nothing living, nothing dying, there is nothing in this world, nothing in the next world, there is nothing now, nothing at the resurrection-morning, nothing in Heaven that is not contained in this text: "I will *never* leave thee; I will *never* forsake thee."

IV. I shall give five blows to drive home the nail while I speak upon

The Sweet Confirmations

of this most precious promise.

1. Let me remind you that the Lord will not and cannot leave His people, because of **His relationship to them**. He is your *Father*; will your Father leave you? Has He not said: "Can a woman forget her sucking child, that she should not have compassion on the son of her womb? yea, they may forget, yet will I not forget thee" (Isa. 49. 15). Would you,

being evil, leave your child to perish? Never, never!
Remember, Christ is your *husband*. Would you, a
husband, neglect your wife? Is it not a shame to a
man, unless he nourisheth and cherisheth her even
as his own body, and will Christ become one of these
ill husbands? Hath He not said: "I hate putting
away," and will He ever put thee away? Remember,
thou art *part of His body*. No man yet ever hated his
own flesh. Thou mayest be but as a little finger, but
will He leave His finger to rot, to perish, to starve?
Thou mayest be the least honourable of all the mem-
bers, but is it not written that upon these He be-
stoweth abundant honour, and so our uncomely parts
have abundant comeliness? If He be Father, if He
be husband, if He be head, if He be all-in-all, how
can He leave thee? Think not so hardly of thy God.

2. Then, next, **His honour** binds Him never to
forsake thee. When we see a house half-built and left
in ruins, we say: "This man began to build and was
not able to finish." Shall this be said of thy God,
that He began to save thee and could not bring thee
to perfection? Is it possible that He will break His
word, and so stain His truth? Shall men be able to
cast a slur upon His power, His wisdom, His love,
His faithfulness? No! thank God, no! "I give,"

saith He, "unto my sheep eternal life, and they shall *never* perish, neither shall any pluck them out of My hand" (John 10. 28).

If thou shouldest perish, believer, Hell would ring with diabolical laughter against the character of God; and if ever one whom Jesus undertook to save should perish, then the demons of the pit would point the finger of scorn for ever against a defeated Christ, against a God that undertook but went not through.

> "His honour is engaged to save
> The meanest of His sheep;
> All that His heavenly Father gave
> His hands securely keep."

3. And if that be not enough, wilt thou remember besides this that **the past** all goes to prove that He will not forsake thee.   Thou hast been in deep waters; hast thou been drowned?   Thou hast walked through the fires; hast thou been burned?   Thou hast had six troubles; hath He forsaken thee?   Thou hast gone down to the roots of the mountains, and the weeds have been wrapped about thy head; hath He not brought thee up again?   Thou hast borne great and sore troubles; but hath He not delivered thee?   Say, when did He leave thee?   Testify against Him; if thou hast found Him forgetful, then doubt Him.   If thou hast found Him unworthy of thy confidence, then

disown Him, but not till then.   The past is vocal with
a thousand songs of gratitude, and every note therein
proveth by an indisputable logic that He will *not*
forsake His people.

4. And if that be not enough ask thy father and
the saints that have gone before.   Did ever any
perish trusting in Christ?   I have heard that some
whom Jehovah loved have fallen from grace, and have
been lost.   He keepeth all His saints; not *one* of them
hath perished; they are in His hand, and have hitherto
been preserved.   David mourneth, "All Thy waves
and Thy billows have gone over me" (Psa. 42. 7);
yet, he crieth, "Hope thou in God, for I shall yet
praise Him."   Jonah laments, "The earth with her
bars was about me for ever;" and yet, ere long he
says, "Salvation is of the Lord" (Jonah 2. 9).   Ye
glorified ones above, through much tribulation ye
have entered the Kingdom, and wearing your white
robes, ye smile from your thrones of glory and say
to us, "Doubt not the Lord, neither distrust Him,
He hath not forsaken His people nor cast off His
chosen."

5. Beloved friends, there is **no reason why He**
should cast us off.   Can you adduce any reason why
He should cast you away?   Is it your poverty, your

nakedness, your peril, the danger of your life? In all these things we are more than conquerors through Him that hath loved us. Do you say it is your sins? Then I answer, sin can never be a cause why God should cast away His people, for they were full of sin when He at first embraced their persons, and espoused their cause. That would have been a cause why He never should have loved them, but having loved them when they were dead in trespasses and sins, their sin can never be a reason for leaving them.

Besides, the Apostle says, "I am persuaded that neither death, nor life, nor angels, nor principalities, nor powers, nor things present, nor things to come"— and sin is one of the things present, and I fear it is one of the things to come—"nor height, nor depth, nor any other creature, shall be able to separate us from the love of God, which is in Christ Jesus our Lord" (Rom. 8. 39).

If there be any truth taught us in Scripture, it is that the children of God cannot perish. If this Book teaches anything whatever, if it be not all a fiction from beginning to end, it teaches in a hundred places that "The righteous *shall hold on his way*, and he that hath clean hands shall be stronger and stronger" (Job 17. 9).

Now, right on our God let us cast the burdens of our bodies, and our souls, for He hath said, "I will never leave thee; I will never forsake thee."

Oh, I wish this promise belonged to you all! I would give my right hand if it could! But some of you must not touch it; it does not belong to some of you, for it is *the exclusive property of the man who trusts in Christ*. "Oh!" saith one, "then I will trust in Christ." Do it, soul, do it; and if thou trustest in Him He will never leave thee. Black as thou art, He will wash thee; He will never leave thee. Wicked as thou art, He will make thee holy; He will never leave thee. Though thou hast nought that should win His love, He will press thee to His bosom; He will *never* leave thee. Living or dying, in time or in eternity, He will never forsake thee, but will surely bring thee to His right hand, and say, "Behold I, and the children whom the Lord hath given Me" (Isa. 8. 18).

May God seal these five negatives upon our memories and hearts for Christ's sake. AMEN.